John Moorman

Michael Manktelow retired from being Bishop of Basingstoke in 1993 and now lives in Chichester, where he is Bursalis Prebendary of the Cathedral and an honorary assistant bishop in the diocese. He is also an honorary assistant bishop in the Diocese of Gibraltar in Europe. He trained for ordination at Chichester Theological College under Dr John Moorman and later served under him in two parishes in the Diocese of Ripon. He is married and has three daughters.

# John Moorman

*Anglican, Franciscan, Independent*

## Michael Manktelow

CANTERBURY
PRESS
Norwich

First published in 1999 by The Canterbury Press Norwich
(a publishing imprint of Hymns Ancient & Modern Limited
a registered charity)
St Mary's Works, St Mary's Plain
Norwich, Norfolk, NR3 3BH

A catalogue record for this book is available
from the British library

ISBN 1-85311-310-7

Typeset by Regent Typesetting, London
and printed in Great Britain by
Biddles Ltd, Guildford and King's Lynn

# Contents

# Preface

John Moorman will be remembered as a Franciscan scholar of international renown; an untiring ecumenist, concerned for truth as much as for unity; and above all as 'an outstanding example of the episcopate of the Church of England at its best'. At once independent and traditional, Catholic and Protestant, his clear grasp of essentials, and courageous expression of them, provides a timely yardstick of classic Anglicanism on this tenth anniversary of his death and at the threshold of the twenty-first century.

Fortunately for his biographer, Moorman left a substantial collection of papers, including biographical sketches of six people who had influenced his life, as well as his diaries which are now in Lambeth Palace Library. Having been encouraged by both Lord Coggan and Professor Henry Chadwick to undertake this work, I have been most grateful for their continuing interest. Many who were Moorman's students at Chichester, or among his clergy in Ripon, or his colleagues in ecumenical work, or friends made in retirement in Durham, have been generous with helpful information and memories. Among these I wish to thank particularly the Right Revds Ralph Emmerson, Edward Knapp-Fisher and Gordon Roe; Professor Howard Root, the Vens Max Godden and John Oliver; Canons John Fenton, Ronnie McFadden, Ted Sheild and Eric Staples; Dom Peter Roundhill, OSB, and the Revds Sir Derek Pattinson, Gordon Dowden, Ben de la Mare and Geoffrey Sowerby; Dr Mary Brown (née Menzies), Miss Gillian Boughton and Miss Virginia Johnstone; the late

Squadron-Leader Peter Driver and Messrs Alan Piper, Roger Till and Don Wilson.

My thanks are also due to the Executors of the late Mary Moorman for permission to quote from letters written by John to her, mostly during the war; to the Master and Fellows of Trinity College, Cambridge, for permission to quote from a letter of G. M. Trevelyan to his brother, R. C. Trevelyan; and to Canon Alan Wilkinson for allowing me to quote from a letter written to him by John. I am grateful also to Dr E. A. Livingstone for helpful advice, particularly in the compilation of the bibliography of John Moorman's writings; Dr Richard Palmer and his staff at Lambeth Palace Library for making John's diaries available for my perusal; Mr Stewart Harper for his word-processing skills; and Mrs Christine Smith of the Canterbury Press.

Finally, to my wife Ros and our three Yorkshire-born daughters who knew and loved John and Mary, I dedicate this book.

Michael Manktelow

Chichester
13 January 1999

# I

# The Making of the Man

John Richard Humpidge Moorman was born in Leeds on 4 June 1905, the second son of Frederic William Moorman and Frances Beatrice Humpidge. His elder brother, Harold, seems to have been something of a black sheep in the family; his life ended in a tragic suicide. John's sister, Theo, was two years younger and was later to become famous for pioneering new techniques in weaving as an art form.[1] Frederic Moorman was Professor of English Language at the University of Leeds and Frances, also a teacher, was to become Warden of Oxley Hall there. The relationship between John and his mother was always particularly close, perhaps because he was not physically strong as a boy.

Being brought up in an academic family, with books around the house and being discussed, meant a liberal and humanist outlook was encouraged in John; at the same time the vigorous life of a great northern city with easy access to some of England's finest countryside in the Yorkshire dales, inculcated a deep love of the north which never left him. Northern independence and scholarly interests thus combined to mould this quintessential Anglican bishop whose life spanned the twentieth century, a century when Franciscan studies exploded, the training of men for the ordained ministry of the Church faced new challenges, and the movement towards the recovery of Christian unity gathered momentum. In any one of these areas John Moorman would have been equipped to play a significant part; in the event he was able to make his mark on them all.

The Moormans were not northerners originally. Rather,

they could trace their roots back to the Isle of Wight, whence one Zechariah Moorman had emigrated to Virginia in 1669, after serving in Cromwell's army. John was proud that this branch of the family had eventually become Quakers, emancipating their slaves and showing concern for their education and welfare. There were also the Moormans of Devon and Cornwall. One of them, Commander Richard Moorman, born in 1784, was to accompany Nelson to the West Indies in 1805, while his nephew Richard, born in 1810, died at Exmouth in 1909 as the oldest Admiral in the world. The latter was John's great-uncle, about whom he learned when a cousin turned up in Chichester with photos and press-cuttings in 1946. 'The old Admiral,' John wrote to his wife Mary, 'was a great radical and incurred a good deal of wrath at the Admiralty by fraternising with the lower deck and trying to get better conditions for the ratings. Rather a jolly old boy, I should think.' John also used to tell of his great-grandmother (d. 1901), who had gone out in a boat from Plymouth harbour in 1815 and seen Napoleon standing on the deck of the *Bellerophon*.

John's grandfather, the Revd Andrew Moorman, was Congregational Minister at Ashburton, Devon, and it was there that Frederic, Andrew's second son, was born in 1872. Frederic graduated at Aberystwyth, which was at that time part of London University, and then went on to Strasbourg to work for a PhD. Although his first published work was a translation of the Rules of Association Football into German, more serious scholarship was displayed in his study entitled *William Browne and the Pastoral Poetry of the Elizabethan Age* (published 1897). Later he was to specialize in Robert Herrick, producing a *Biography and Critical Study* in 1910 and the definitive edition of his poetical works five years later.

Returning from Strasbourg after two years, Frederic became Lecturer in English at Aberystwyth; there he met Frances Humpidge whom he was to marry. Frances was helping her sister-in-law Johanna to run a Dame School in the town. Johanna was a German who had married Frances's brother Tom, a Professor at Aberystwyth, and after his early death she started her small school. John recalls meeting this formidable lady and being fascinated to see a portrait of Johannes Brahms on her piano. He was even more amazed to learn that her family had expected her to marry the great composer. 'My aunt nearly married Brahms,' he used to enjoy telling people, adding, 'but if she had she would not have been my aunt!'

In 1898 Frederic moved to a lectureship at the Yorkshire College at Leeds. This became a university six years later and Frederic was eventually made Professor in 1913. John remembered his father as 'a most loveable man who was far too modest to fight for the recognition he deserved'. At Leeds, Frederic developed a consuming interest in Yorkshire dialect and literature. Cycling round the dales with a dictaphone, he recorded the actual speech of folk who lived in remote hamlets and dwellings. In publishing his *West Riding Place Names* in 1910, he expressed the belief that the chief value of place-name study lay on the side of history, not philology: 'Our English place-names, when they have been adequately investigated, county by county, will do much to illuminate what is still to a large extent obscure – the origins of the English people and the foundations of English society.' He followed this up with *Yorkshire Dialect Poems* (1916) and *Tales, Songs and Plays of the Ridings*, published posthumously five years later.

John inherited his father's fascination with Yorkshire folk and speech, and was to write later of 'a respect for the English language which was sensitive to the shock of hearing it badly spoken, like a violinist or a singer going out of tune'. From his father, too, he learned the art of bird-watching, and like him used to record in his diaries the birds he had seen. He and Theo would cycle up the dales with their father on bird-watching expeditions, and then in the summer the whole family would go up to their cottage at Hawkswick in Littondale. It was there, on Frederic's forty-seventh birthday, 8 September 1919, that tragedy struck the family. As John was later to recall:

September 8 was a warm and sunny day and it was decided

in the afternoon that my father should take his younger
children for a bathe in the River Skirfare. When we got there
my father jumped into the water and called to my sister,
Theo, to follow him. She leapt cheerfully into the pool, but
almost immediately got into difficulties and started shouting
for help. At this point I realized that my father had
completely disappeared until I discovered, to my horror,
that he was lying motionless, on his back, at the bottom of
the pool. My father was dead.

Perhaps the coldness of the water affected what was known to
be a weak heart, but the shattering of an idyllic holiday and
the traumatic effect it inevitably had on the whole family – not
least this young lad of 14 – was something of which John never
spoke in later life. He had already won an open scholarship to
Gresham's School, Holt, Norfolk, and it was here that he was
to start just two weeks later.

Gresham's had been founded in 1555 as a country grammar
school, becoming a public boarding school in 1900. Under
the headship of George Howson it quickly acquired a good
reputation, attracting the sons of Oxbridge families like
Gooch, Murray and Lindsay, and also including among its
pupils around that time Spender, Auden and Britten. Not only
did the headmaster have imagination and flair, but the school
itself was free from what John would call 'the less admirable
characteristics of many of the older public schools'. For
example, he was horrified to read in later life about the
cruelty and vice which C. S. Lewis had spoken of in his
*Surprised by Joy*. Instead, Gresham's inculcated a moral code
alongside the encouragement of individual personality. It was,
he said, 'A school where your maiden aunt could live for a
term without being shocked'. John responded well to this free
and healthy environment which gave scope for the development of a boy's natural interests and also gave plenty of leisure
time for reading. It was during these years that he read most
of the classic English novels, particularly devouring those of

Charles Dickens and Thomas Hardy. Too much time, he thought, was spent in compulsory games and the cadet corps. The latter he deemed quite unnecessary now that the war was over. Moreover, 'war is a sin', he somewhat naively recorded in his schoolboy diary. Nevertheless he made the summer camp with the corps more tolerable by forming a little dance orchestra with piano, violins, cornet, drum and two 'swanee whistles'. Thus one of his contemporaries at Gresham's was to write to Mary at the time of John's death that 'people might think from his ecclesiastical and theological career that he was a solemn fellow, but he was quite the opposite, light in touch and enjoying many unserious pleasures, like hockey, fell-walking and Gilbert and Sullivan'.

Above all at Gresham's John learned 'that secret of all communication between individuals, especially those of different ages: the power to understand, to feel, to give oneself wholly to the other person without any touch of condescension or patronage'. In this regard he had been particularly fortunate to have Walter Greatorex as his music master.[2] 'The school was his life', John was to write in an unpublished sketch later. 'It was to him what a religious community is to a man living under life vows. It was a world of its own with its own language, its own jokes, its joys and sorrows, successes and tragedies.' Both Auden and Spender were later to testify to Greatorex's gift for friendship, but for John there was the additional encouragement that Greatorex gave to his musical proclivities. They played Bach and Beethoven together, agreeing that the latter's last quartets were the greatest of music's masterpieces, and then Greatorex would daringly launch into Scriabin. 'He was a perfectionist and that made him want others to discover and produce all that was beautiful'; an educator of taste, a quiet enthusiast and a great entertainer.

It was while studying at Gresham's that John began to keep a diary. Starting on 1 January 1921 it was to be a daily record of his doings, books read, and plants and birds seen. His recorded weight then of 6 stone 12 pounds and height of 5 foot 2½ inches did not increase very significantly in his subsequent lifetime, for he always remained slight of stature. He was constantly bright-eyed like a bird, taking in quickly all that he saw around him, and boyish to the end in his enthusiasm and pride of achievement.

The diaries were maintained with nearly 18,000 entries over a period of 67 years. These cannot be compared in quantity or substance with Mr Gladstone's almost 26,000 entries written daily over 70 years, nor even with Pope John XXIII's *Journal of a Soul* written from the age of 15 to 81. Of the latter John was to comment, 'But the sort of thing he was writing at the age of fifteen is very similar to what he wrote when he was 80.'[3] In spite of all the Pope's experience in different lands, 'he continued to live in what must be described as a very small world, reading the same devotional books over and over again, thinking the same thoughts, going through the same devotional exercises'. John's diaries, by contrast, developed into a valuable record of his outward activities, as well as the innermost thoughts of a man who was never idle nor too introspective. At each year's end, however, he would take stock of himself. 'I feel that I am getting much older and wiser,' he wrote on 31 December 1923. 'I think more about the world and life in general.' Thus in his nineteenth year he began to think more seriously about his life and what he would do with it. He read Ramsay MacDonald on *The Socialist Movement* and came to regard Socialism as 'a high ideal which will soon be predominant', and he even made the first of a lifetime's contributions to the *Yorkshire Post* by writing about unemployment.

At the same time his idealism was even more fired by reading for the first time *The Little Flowers of St Francis*, which his mother had given him, adding 'I think you will like it'. So John confided to his diary, 'If only there were a few St Francises in the world today', adding somewhat piously, 'Sometimes I seriously think of giving up the world.' He acknowledged, however, that it might be harder to do so in the twentieth century than in the thirteenth. But a sermon which he heard around this time in the school chapel on the life of a parish priest was to sow a seed which developed richly, though his immediate comment was merely that here was 'a very fine occupation for a man, but I think a priest ought not to marry'.

With all this uppermost in his mind John went up to Emmanuel College, Cambridge, in October 1924 to read history, feeling that he would not 'go in for law but religion' and that 'the Church provided the calling best fitted to my temperament'. He spoke to the Dean, Henry Burnaby,[4] who 'clearly advised me to do so, though he never urged people into it', while the University Mission Week in February 1926, conducted by William Temple (then Bishop of Manchester), 'made me more determined than ever to take Holy Orders and I think I am as certain as one can be'. He continued, 'I owe a very deep debt to the Mission but it is one I can only pay by carrying out to the best of my abilities the precepts laid down in the Christian religion. May God help me.'

He found lectures on constitutional history very dry, but had an exciting Director of Studies in Edward Welbourne, later Master of his College, and an inspiring teacher in G. G. Coulton. The latter's passionate concern for people and for truth had great appeal for him; it led him on to read Coulton's *Christ, St Francis and Today* as well as to attend the course of lectures that he was giving on St Francis and the Franciscans. John thought that he might himself write a short life of Francis, having by this time devoured the works of G. K. Chesterton, Sabatier and Fr Cuthbert on the subject, as well as St Bonaventure's *Life*. He asked of the latter how much was fact or fiction, commenting, 'If one tenth is true, St Francis must have been not only a very wonderful man but indeed almost a second Jesus Christ. The main difference between the two is that Jesus Christ called himself the Son of God and St Francis called himself a vile sinner.' Having joined the British Society of Franciscan Studies, John now founded the Cambridge Franciscan Society on similar lines. This was in time to mark the seven-hundredth anniversary in 1926 of St Francis's death. Professor F. C. Burkitt[5] agreed to be president while John acted as secretary. Speakers at their meetings included Fr Cuthbert OFMCap and Dr G. G. Coulton. John owed much to Burkitt's friendship and encouragement, and when the Professor died John wrote, 'It seemed to make no difference that one was at the top of the scholastic tree, and the other was at the bottom.'

'With such devotion to Franciscan studies,' John wrote 40 years later,[6] 'I naturally longed to go to Assisi and if possible other places connected with St Francis. But I had not much hope of doing this. Facilities for students to travel abroad were not nearly as good then as they are now.' But in 1928 Professor Burkitt gave him a cheque for £25: 'Enough then to pay my fare [to Assisi] and give me three weeks there.' Straightaway John found an elderly lady in Cambridge to give him Italian lessons and off he went on what was to be the first of almost annual pilgrimages to the Franciscan holy places. Staying at the Convento San Quirico, and speaking only Italian at meals, John was known there as 'Giovannino' ('Little John'). 'During those three weeks I walked about Assisi until I knew every street, every flight of steps, every church and almost every house. And all the time I was thinking about St Francis. Did he walk down this street, or go through that gate?' Sadly Sabatier, who had done so much in the previous 30 years to arouse the modern interest in St Francis and had himself lived much in Assisi – as greatly loved there as John himself was later to become – had died four years earlier, so John never met him. But Assisi itself was still very much a medieval Umbrian hill-town, untrammelled by the visitors who swarm there today and unharmed, too, by the earthquakes which have more recently caused such damage to its basilica, with its frescoes of the saint.

Refreshed by this visit John returned to Cambridge, switching from history to theology in the Tripos and then moving across from Emmanuel to Westcott House for his ordination training. Here he felt completely at home. 'The last thing one could call the place would be a seminary – it was scarcely a college,' he wrote. 'It was rather like a perpetual reading-party organized by some human and deeply beloved college don.' That man was B. K. Cunningham, who had been Principal of the House since 1919. Before the First World War he, together with T. G. Gardiner, had been involved under Bishop Randall Davidson in the Farnham Brotherhood in the preparation of 'English gentlemen in Holy Orders'. Cunningham's genius for friendship and for winning affection and loyalty led to the creation of 'a new kind of community', John reflected. Each student was free to develop 'his own best self as God intended', within the common life of the college and was not required to conform to a pattern or type. 'It is quite amazing,' he wrote, 'what power and educative value this common life possesses, given any group of men who meet with aims in common.'

John revelled equally in the absence of party labels in the college and 'the reverence for the largeness and majesty of Truth' which pervaded the place. Above all, B. K.'s (Cunningham) dictum – 'Let the order of growth be first that which is natural and afterwards that which is spiritual' – remained with him when he in turn became Principal of the Theological College at Chichester and later expanded that responsibility for clergy as Bishop of Ripon. He liked to quote B. K.'s comment that 'Perhaps the greatest weakness of Church of England clergy today is not that there are a few men who ought never to have been priests, but that there are many priests who have never been men... Do not begin by building the priest: begin with the man and draw out the best that is in each.' Paramount, however, in the Westcott ethos was the minimum of discipline imposed from without, together with a maximum 'suggested and worked out from within'. That self-discipline – σωφρονισμός – which had been the key to B. K.'s ministry was undoubtedly to become the mainspring of John's own.

## Notes

1. Theo Moorman, *Weaving as an Art Form: A Personal Statement*, (Van Nostrand Reinhold, New York, 1975).

2. Greatorex is now best known for his hymn tune, 'Woodlands'.
3. '"His Name was John": Some Reflections on the "Journal of a Soul"', *The Heythrop Journal*, (October 1965).
4. Brother of John, who was to become Regius Professor of Divinity at Cambridge, and of Davy, the music hall artist.
5. Norris-Hulse Professor of Divinity at Cambridge University.
6. 'Assisi after Forty Years' in *The New Franciscan*, 1.9 (September 1968).

# 2

# Early Ministry

*Leeds*

John was ordained deacon on Trinity Sunday, 26 May 1929, by Bishop Arthur Burroughs in Ripon Cathedral. He served his title at St Matthew's Holbeck, a working-class parish of some 10,000 people in south Leeds. Covering an area of less than a square mile, it had retained its 'village' character, but with considerable overcrowding in back-to-back houses. These had only one bedroom and one living room, no indoor sanitation and barely any backyard. Houses opened out on to the street and the washing was hung out on ropes across the street. Here John was brought face to face with the realities of life and death, and above all the grit and humour of Yorkshire folk. They earthed him in his ministry and he never forgot them.

The vicar of the parish was Canon R. J. Wood; Philip Simpson, later to be Rector of Adel, was the senior curate. Both were to become lifelong friends, and in due course when John had become their bishop, he visited them in their declining years and eventually buried them. There were also parishioners with whom John kept in touch until their lives' end: Kitty Burns in particular was one whom he held in fondest memory. She was the illegitimate daughter of a 'toff', was married to the local coalman and so knew well the households in greatest need. She not only 'presided' at the tea-urn at social functions but also frequently acted both as midwife and layer-out – 'liggin' in and liggin' aht' as she called it. 'Without education, money or influence,' John wrote, 'she was able to do a vast amount of good in a community suffering from the effects of unemployment and neglect.'

For the clergy the day began at 6.45 am in church with Mass, Mattins and intercessions. Once a week John enjoyed teaching in the schools: 'I often think I am a teacher by birth,' he wrote. In the mornings he was usually able to work at his desk, reading Celano, perhaps, or books like Creighton's *Life and Letters*, as well as preparing talks and sermons. He was distressed when he could not baptize a stillborn baby, seeing that problem as 'one of the most tragic and inexplicable that there is'. And while he enjoyed being with cubs, scouts and rovers, he regarded the Juniors' Club as his 'weekly penance' and the Seniors' Club 'entirely alien', with their vulgar songs like 'I ain't never been kissed'.

His sensitivity here was doubtless due to his just having become engaged to Mary Caroline Trevelyan that autumn. While walking and bird-watching together in Wharfedale they had come, he records in his diary,

> to a most lovely little wood – very wild, where it seemed as if man had never been before. There was a delicious little beck gurgling and singing to us, and the sun was shining through the trees, making great splashes of bright light on the tree trunks and on the ground. Here, in this lovely place, we became engaged in circumstances that could not have been more romantic.

With his accustomed reticence, however, he goes on, 'As this diary is a record of events and not of emotions I shall not attempt to say what my feelings are even if it were possible to do so. Therefore I shall just leave this bare narrative as it is and the rest to the imagination.'

Mary assured John that there would be no difficulty informing her parents, who had been 'anticipating and eagerly hoping for it for some time'. It was to be a marriage into that 'intellectual aristocracy' of which Lord Annan has written in a fascinating essay.[1] Mary's father was George Macaulay Trevelyan, whose descent from Lord Macaulay, the great historian, was given new impetus by his own appointment to

be Regius Professor of Modern History, as well as Master of
Trinity College, at Cambridge. Her mother, Janet Penrose
Ward, was the daughter of Mrs Humphrey Ward, the novelist,
who in her turn was the grand-daughter of Dr Thomas Arnold
of Rugby and niece of Matthew Arnold, the poet. John commented after reading Janet's life of her mother that Mrs
Humphrey Ward and her grand-daughter had 'much in common'. A few weeks later he went with Mary and her mother to
Italy for his post-Christmas break.

Mary's admiration of her father can be observed in her own
memoir of him.[2] But if this seems to come close to idolization,
it may equally have been the inevitable result of her mother's
overwhelming grief at losing the elder of her sons, Theodore.
He was only five years old when he died after an operation for
appendicitis. This tragedy seemed to prevent Janet from giving
to her daughter that warmth and affection that she craved.
This surely had a bearing on Mary's own emotional development and perhaps gives a clue to her adulthood when she
seemed both to need the physical demonstration of affection
and yet to shrink from it. John's own reticence and self-
discipline failed to unlock her passionate side, so their
marriage was primarily an intellectual companionship. 'This is
Mr Moorman and this is Miss Trevelyan and they are going to
amalgamate', was how Mrs Burkitt introduced the happy
couple to her friends in Cambridge after their engagement. But
sadly the amalgamation did not lead to parenthood and
their later years were deprived of that extra dimension which
family life can give.

Mary's father was clearly delighted with the match. 'He
belongs as much to the academic as to the clerical world,' he
wrote about his son-in-law. 'His views are liberal-minded, and
I have talked about religion and history with him with much
agreement, and no feeling of barrier such as I should feel with
a narrow-minded parson or an Anglo-Catholic.' Then, highest
accolade of all, 'He is a fine walker, and has walked his fifty
miles.'[3] As an 'Anglican agnostic', G. M. Trevelyan was doubtless helped by John to take an increasingly well-disposed view

of the Church of England. He described himself as 'A flying
buttress of the Church: I support it, but from the outside'.
Undoubtedly this relationship made John very sensitive to the
need for the Church in its services to provide for these 'seekers
after Truth' who were not yet, and perhaps never would be,
communicant members of it. There should always be a place
for Mattins, well sung in its Prayer Book form, and with a
thoughtful sermon. Significantly one of his favourite texts
throughout his own preaching ministry was Psalm 69:6, 'Let
not them that trust in thee, O Lord God of hosts, be ashamed
for my cause: let not those that seek thee be confounded
through me, O Lord God of Israel.'

John and Mary were married on Michaelmas Day,
29 September 1930, in Trinity College Chapel, Cambridge, by
Dr Murray, the former Master of Selwyn College and a
family friend, and Dr Stewart, the Dean of Trinity. The hymn
'*Discendi, Amor santo*' ('Come down, O love divine') by
Bianco da Siena, which was considerably less well known then,
was sung by the congregation and Bach's 'Jesu, joy of man's
desiring' by the chapel choir. The register was signed in the
ante-chapel under the statue of Lord Macaulay. After a recep-
tion at the Trevelyans' house in West Road, the couple left for
three weeks in Italy, travelling by train. The first few days were
spent in Florence, where they 'feasted [their] eyes on the Fra
Angelicos', and then on to Assisi for the feast of St Francis on
4 October. Although there were crowds in the Lower Church,
John felt that in this most special of places 'for a time the
world is lost and we seem to come very near to God – the sort
of place, like the Garden of Eden, where God delights to walk
in the cool of the evening and one seems to understand things
hidden from the wise and prudent'. Moving on to Arezzo they
were able to complete their pilgrimage by going up to La
Verna, where St Francis had received the stigmata. On the
return journey home they got into the wrong half of the train
at Bologna, and so were taken to Venice instead of Milan. The
sight of so much water was the first indication for the honey-
mooners of their unfortunate mistake, and it took all of John's

skill in Italian to prevent the ticket collector from charging them for their wrong journey. They nevertheless had to pay for their subsequent journey from Venice to Milan, where they caught the night train to Paris, and thence back home.

## Leighton Buzzard

After four years at Holbeck, it was time for John to move to his second curacy at Leighton Buzzard, for which he had been strongly recommended by B. K. Cunningham. It was a wrench to leave the Leeds folk among whom he had been so happy. 'In four years,' he noted in his diary, 'I have preached 342 times (including the workhouse and other churches), baptized 205 babies, married 55 couples and taken 302 funerals. I have visited 683 houses.' The new parish was a complete contrast: after his first Sunday there he wrote, 'I find people here very polite and very friendly, but not so familiar as the Holbeck people. They all call me "sir", and the men take off their hats to me in the street. No one did that at Holbeck.' The stiffer southern atmosphere contrasted with the more down-to-earth north, and John and Mary were not happy in what they later called 'those strange two years'.

John's new vicar was Canon S. E. Swann, who had previously been Chaplain of Trinity Hall, Cambridge, then an archdeacon first in Nairobi and later in Egypt. He had only come to Leighton Buzzard earlier that year and had already engaged D. B. McGregor, a contemporary of John's at Westcott, to be his other curate. Although he liked Swann at first, quite early on John felt he sat too lightly to the job, playing golf several times a week and even taking time off to coach one of the Trinity Hall boats. He also felt that Swann was too casual about the Sacrament. When the Vicar brought John Holy Communion at home when he was ill, he only used the Prayer of Humble Access before communicating him, saying the Lord's Prayer, the Gloria and the Blessing afterwards. 'I should have considered I'd failed in my duty if I gave any sick communicant less than the Collect, Epistle and Gospel, the

Invitation, Confession and Absolution, and the Prayer of Humble Access before Communion,' John wrote as a result. Then one Sunday he was shocked to see Swann administering two chalices at once, one in each hand. When John tackled him about it at the staff meeting, the Vicar expressed surprise that anyone should have such scruples. A few months later John openly contradicted him at a Finance Committee meeting, admitting that there was now 'no confidence on either side and the sooner the partnership is dissolved the better'.

Nevertheless John's time at Leighton Buzzard was fruitful. He started a scout troop and worked hard in preparing boys for Confirmation. He would see each of them individually, helping them towards self-examination and confession. To this end he drew up a scheme based on St Paul's 'fruit of the Spirit' in Galatians 5, later publishing it in *Theology*.[4] On a clean sheet of paper three columns were drawn: in the first were listed 'love, joy, peace, longsuffering, gentleness, goodness, faithfulness, meekness, self-control'; in the second, the question 'What does this mean to you?' was addressed; and in the third, the opposites were recorded. Each boy measured himself up to these, with the majority proceeding to make a sacramental confession. John commended it as a scheme based on the Bible, which is 'the normal textbook of the Christian disciple'; moreover its emphasis lay on the positive virtue rather than the sin which was to be regarded as falling short of the ideal. Less edifying, however, was a Servers' Guild service, which John criticized savagely. The plainsong was execrable, and such 'worship' must be a trial to God, who would surely want to bring the church 'crashing about their ears'. He particularly disliked seeing priests in their birettas smoking cigarettes, and was genuinely concerned at the real harm he felt was being done by Anglo-Catholics who aped Rome and whom he felt were not sufficiently concerned about the Kingdom of God. He had been equally dismissive of Rotarians when taken as a guest to their weekly luncheon, disliking in particular their 'general air of extreme heartiness'.

Two events in the autumn of 1933, however, gave him great

encouragement. The first was when he joined with a team of missioners to St Peter's Blackburn under the leadership of Christopher Turner, the Vicar of St Aidan's Leeds, whom he so much admired. At the outset of the mission John made his own first confession to him: 'I felt God very near to us,' he wrote in his diary. John was then responsible for the children's side of the mission, though he felt that 15 days was too long a time for this and questioned what they were really trying to do. However, he played his accordion to good effect and the children continued to attend.

The second was the visit of Brother Douglas of the Society of St Francis. John thought his sermon was 'about the most impressive thing I have ever heard'. The congregation was likewise moved by its simplicity and its pathos, combined with thankfulness for the work which was being done for 'down and outs' at the Home of St Francis at nearby Hatfield. John was to write more fully about the deep impression Brother Douglas made upon himself in one of his unpublished portraits. He saw this priest, who could have continued to live comfortably as a college chaplain in Oxford, as one who, like St Francis, truly lived by the precepts of the Gospel. In the twentieth century he was doing for the poor, the unemployed, the vagrant and the verminous what St Francis himself had done in the thirteenth century, thereby teaching the world that its sense of values was wrong and that persons, even when regarded as scum, were of greater significance than power, privilege and security.

One of the very early biographers of St Francis called him the 'Mirror of Perfection'. Brother Douglas would have been horrified and appalled if anyone had said that of him. Yet some of us, in those far off days, felt that in him we had found a quality and fullness of Christian love and dedication which we never quite found again.'[5]

## Manchester

After six years in Orders and two very different curacies, John was more than ready to move on. Three very different possibilities presented themselves in the summer of 1934: a living in Norfolk, which John saw as being 'a ducal village' like neighbouring Woburn; the senior curacy of St Aidan's Leeds, where he would be working with the priest with whom he had already been on the Blackburn mission, Christopher Turner; and the chaplaincy of Bradfield School. However, what he really wanted was to have his own parish where he could order the worship, try out his ideas, and even train his own curates. B. K. Cunningham suggested the possibility of a parish in Manchester and John went up to see it in February 1935. 'It is one of the most important parishes in the Manchester district,' Cunningham wrote. 'There could be offered you no more influential job in the north – but it must be a BIG decision – it is no jumping-off place – eight years at least I should say, and your life's best work. So go, and God bless you and plenty of power to your arm!' When interviewed by the five lay trustees, he was asked, 'Are you a high churchman or a low churchman, or a sort of 'appy medium?' Then, 'You appear to be a very young man. Are you a good preacher?' John thought of the prophet Jeremiah, 'Ah! Lord God, behold I do not know how to speak, for I am only a youth. (Jer. 1:6)' Then on accepting, he prayed that 'I may build and be built up'.

Holy Innocents, Fallowfield, was a residential parish in south Manchester, with a Tractarian tradition. It was close to the University and had one of the halls of residence in it. Its population of 8000 was mixed, comprising many living in back-to-back terraced houses and some professional people in more substantial houses. Although the country as a whole was at that time still recovering from the great depression of the early 1930s, there was little unemployment in Fallowfield itself. The previous incumbent had an outgoing personality and was very popular, while his wife, as the daughter of a

Manchester professor, had been regarded by the professional people in the parish as one of themselves. Mary undoubtedly had the appropriate academic background but her somewhat abrupt, and at times outspoken, manner was not so easily appreciated. John, however, quickly won the hearts of the people by his loving pastoral care and personal holiness. Together John and Mary were generous in their hospitality at the rectory, not least on Sunday evenings when curate and organist were invited to supper, followed by music-making on two pianos. Manchester as a city was ideally suited to them both: there was the Rylands Library where they could consult the books they needed for their own writing; there were the Hallé concerts which they attended regularly; and it was easy to get up to the Lake District where they enjoyed walking and bird-watching. John also went climbing and would take two or three youths from the parish with him to tackle Scafell Pike. Canon Ted Sheild, who was one of his curates, writes, 'It may have been due to his own small physique that he had such a great admiration for feats of physical endurance. His special hero was Scott of the Antarctic and he even dressed like him on some of his climbing excursions.'[6] He particularly recalls a memorable occasion when John posed for a snapshot dressed in this way in front of the small tent which he and the boys had pitched on the snow line.

Ted Sheild was a New Zealander who had been looking for a curacy in England before returning to his own country. B. K. Cunningham advised him to look at two parishes: one was large and in the south of England, with an experienced vicar; the other was Fallowfield with its new, young incumbent. Ted's chaplain at Oxford, E. C. Ratcliff, remembered John from Westcott days as 'a nice young man who played the virginals' and recommended Sheild to go to the older man. That incumbent, however, could not wait beyond the Trinity ordination, so Ted recalls that when he telephoned Fallowfield rectory it was Mary who answered in John's absence. She 'peremptorily summoned' him to appear at the rectory that very weekend. On arrival, however, he was met at the door by 'a quiet little man even smaller than myself'. He was offered the title and ordained deacon at Michaelmas.

'From the start,' Sheild writes, 'John treated me as a partner rather than a trainee curate. We were close in age, only five years between us. We had widely different backgrounds, but we shared the same ideals and had the same priorities concerning our ministry.' So they 'shared everything that could be shared' – preaching, Confirmation preparation, visiting. For the latter they would meet at the rectory in mid-afternoon, where Ted would find John in his study, sitting in a low chair with a writing-board across his knees, working on his Franciscan studies or furthering his knowledge of Italian. He used to do this for an hour or so after lunch every day. They would then set out together on their house-to-house visitation of the parish.

Early in his time at Fallowfield John set out what was needed for the parish to go forward. 'The first need was more sustained prayer, the second was a greater fellowship among the parishioners themselves (for church-people are more likely to squabble than anyone else), and the third was that all should be more conscious that Fallowfield was a very, very small part of God's Kingdom.' On one occasion, after commending the church organizations for the work they were doing, John added,

> But I shall never cease trying to impress upon you how absolutely vital it is that we should put spiritual things first. The Church exists for the worship of God and the building up of his Kingdom in the hearts of men; it is not an organisation to provide cheap amenities for the general public.

John was fond, too, of giving his definition of a Christian, who is, as he taught his Confirmation candidates, 'A person who worships God as revealed by Jesus and who is consciously trying to be like Christ'. This was stressed in his preaching and was the high standard that he demanded of himself. He expected it also in his fellow clergy and was ruthless in his criticism of 'busy little men', popularists and show preachers always seeking advancement. As a junior incumbent, he even took 'the platform' at the Diocesan Conference to task, accusing them of getting their priorities wrong.

War clouds, however, were gathering during the Fallowfield period. In the Far East, Japan was expanding aggressively; and nearer home the Spanish Civil War aroused deep concern, for here an internal conflict was in danger of being turned into a major conflagration. There was considerable anti-fascist feeling against Franco and volunteers went from England to fight. Others were active in providing help for Spanish refugees, and John was among those who organized gifts of clothing and medical aid for children who had been placed in a home near Bolton. Neville Chamberlain's visit to Hitler in Munich (1938) came as a respite in the growing tension, and Sheild comments on what might otherwise be seen as a wholehearted pacifism on John's part: 'His strong opposition to a military solution was not so much because of the dreadful carnage and the wholesale destruction brought about by war, but more the effect it had on the mind and spirit both individually and collectively. The values and ideals of the Sermon on the Mount were always uppermost in his thinking.' So too, we could add, was the spirit of St Francis.

## Notes

1. 'The Intellectual Aristocracy' in J. H. Plumb (ed.), *Studies in Social History: A Tribute to G. M. Trevelyan*, Longmans, Green, 1955.
2. Mary Moorman, *George Macaulay Trevelyan: A Memoir*, Hamish Hamilton, 1980.
3. See David Cannadine, *G. M. Trevelyan: A Life in History*, Harper Collins, 1992, p. 37.
4. *Theology*, 28. 165 (March 1934), pp. 165-7.
5. *Good Without Pretence: Six Portraits in One Frame*, (unpublished).
6. Letter to author.

# 3

# 'Cassock and Corduroy'

The outbreak of the Second World War in September 1939 disturbed John deeply. He had always recognized an innate pacifism within himself, but acknowledged that the belligerence of Nazi Germany must be checked. Pastoral work in the parish must continue and there was a new sense of urgency to get his book entitled *Church Life in England in the Thirteenth Century* completed. But two things particularly worried him: one was how responsible Christians should pray during the conflict; the other was his own personal contribution to the war effort as an able-bodied male in his mid-thirties.

The first matter became particularly worrying when Days of Prayer were commended by Church leaders, although he agreed with the then Archbishop of York, William Temple, that 'the spirit in which we fight, matters more than our winning'. John felt that the form of service issued in May 1940 had trust in God as its keynote and was right to pray that our forces 'whether by life or by death might win for the whole world the fruits of their sacrifice and a holy peace'. Ten months later, however, the burden of the service had become 'a passionate prayer that God will give us victory over our enemies'. Psalms of imprecation and revenge (3 and 5) had now been chosen instead of those such as 20, 27, 46 and 121, which conveyed 'the idea of courage and of the peace and power which come from living close to God'. Thus he wrote about 'An unworthy form of service' to the Editor of *Theology* on 26 March 1941 in the strongest possible terms, castigating this

betrayal of Christ by the Churches... What I cannot forgive

is the fact that the Church has allowed itself to be infected by the evil and damnable spirit which, like a cancer, is eating into people's minds all around us... There is the tragedy, greater than the destruction of our homes, greater than the destruction of our churches, greater even than would be the defeat of what we are fighting for.

The betrayal was not only of Christ, but also of 'those who are striving, against almost overwhelming odds, to keep the flame of sanity and charity alive in the hearts of men'.[1]

Secondly, as the war went on, John felt increasingly uncomfortable with being in an exempted occupation. As an ordained minister he could not, of course, have been a combatant, but he did not feel called even to be a chaplain in one of the armed forces. 'I suppose I am really a pacifist. I couldn't kill anyone; I couldn't be a chaplain to those who were killing people all the time', he wrote many years later to Alan Wilkinson who had mentioned John's stand in his book *Dissent or Conform?*[2] Yet he yearned to do something that was more directly related to the war-effort, and as a start he decided in March 1942 'to devote my day off each week to work on the land'. At first this meant working at Donner House, on a local estate, as an assistant gardener. 'I see you've got a boy. Where did you get him?' asked an envious neighbour in those days of labour shortage.

At the same time he was working in the John Rylands Library putting the finishing touches to his book on the thirteenth-century Church. In his diary on 14 August he wrote, 'I came home in triumph. It was a curious feeling to have finished off a piece of work which has occupied so much of my time and thought.' It was submitted to Cambridge for the Doctorate of Divinity, which was eventually awarded three years later. Then on the next day, 15 August 1942, Bishop Alwyn Williams of Durham wrote to offer John the post of Diocesan Director of Education. But he was much troubled by this possibility of preferment when so many of his friends and contemporaries were having to give up so much. It did not seem right that the clergy should be exempt from making such a sacrifice. 'A cross is being offered to the world', he wrote, 'and everyone is taking it up except the very people who ought to have been the first to accept it.' Young men returning from the war would see the clergy as having sheltered behind their exemption. As his share in the common sacrifice, therefore, he finally decided on 24 August to work full time on the land, on a private's pay.

The very next day, another Bishop Williams – this time 'burglar Bill' of Carlisle – offered John 'the one job in the world that I really wanted – Windermere', where he would succeed his old friend Maurice Harland, who was to become Bishop of Croydon. So on 28 August John went to see his own bishop in Manchester, Guy Warman, and was 'pleasantly surprised at his reaction'. He agreed that neither the Durham post nor the Cumbrian parish were quite right at that juncture, and John was immensely relieved to have his support when Warman realized that going to work on the land was 'a matter of conscience and not a whim'. At the same time he was surprised to be told 'that I was one of the very few people in the world with real powers of leadership though I think that I may have a streak of originality'. Subsequent history judges that in fact he had both.

The next hurdle was to inform his Church Council of his decision, which he did on 7 September. They expressed 'not one word of doubt or criticism', and John felt this to be 'a spiritual experience, making me feel that the efforts of the last seven years have not been in vain'. Asked by one member whether he would wear khaki, he replied, 'No, corduroy.' Eighteen months later he was to produce 200 pages of typescript on his experience of working on the land, entitling it *Cassock and Corduroy*. Mary thought the title 'vulgar' and two different publishers turned it down in December 1943.

John's last Sunday at Fallowfield was 27 September 1942 and he was able to look back on seven very happy years in the parish 'with pleasure and affection'. He had experienced much loyalty and friendship there and he added that 'We've really explored some of the mysteries of God'. Two days later, on Michaelmas Day (which was also the twelfth anniversary of his marriage to Mary), he started work as an agricultural labourer. The bishop, however, required John to sign a deed of resignation, much to the consternation of the Church Council who felt that this was a complete volte-face. John, too, wondered why he was being asked to do this when other clergy going off to the war were permitted to keep their benefices. 'Guy has gone back on his word,' he wrote. But more seriously, now that the rectory had to be vacated, where was Mary going to live? It had been decided that she would stay on in Manchester to teach and she eventually got a post as a history teacher at Broughton High School in Salford, while a villa in Amherst Road was found where she could live and where all John's books could be housed. Above all, Mary was to receive immense support at this difficult period from her great-aunt Annie[3] at The Park, a large house on the outskirts of Prestwich where many involved in public service found a congenial meeting-place.

John had anticipated that there would be certain difficulties in finding a job on the land. In the first place, farm work, far from being something that can be tackled at sight, is in fact a highly skilled occupation to be mastered only after years of experience. Secondly, although the clergy had once been close to the soil, farming their own glebe, those days had gone. Moreover, there was a certain distance between the parson and the working man, which could cause a feeling of suspicion and even embarrassment. Clergy were thought to be easily shocked by strong language and bad habits, and were even seen to be anxious to prevent people from enjoying themselves. 'Consequently,' John wrote, 'while recognizing the parson's general usefulness in his own sphere, and while paying him the respect due to his position in the community, they would be a little reluctant to have such a man working for them and living in the house.' Farmers might be afraid of hiring a parson for fear that their other men would leave. So, instead of advertising for a post or responding to such an advertisement

– which would have entailed explaining why he was exempt from military service – John applied to the War Agricultural Committee in Cumbria, saying that in order to get a footing he would be prepared to work for a trial month, if necessary without pay and only asking for his keep.

The chairman replied offering three jobs: one at Grasmere, which John felt was too much associated with holidaying; another at a camp for Italian prisoners near Penrith, which would have given him too much status and authority as a kind of foreman (though he admitted that the prospect of working and talking with Italians was attractive); and a third which was at Heanings Farm, Musgrave, near Kirkby Stephen, where he would be working for a couple of months doing a 54-hour week. John chose the third job. This involved starting at 8 am and finishing at 6 pm, with an hour off for meals, from Monday to Saturday. Sundays, however, were completely free and he was glad to help the Vicar, MacLeod Murray, who had two churches to look after, with three services every Sunday in each, including sermons or addresses.

The farm work was hard and unfamiliar; unfamiliar, too, was the experience of living *en famille* with the 'hind', or farm manager and his wife. Even more unfamiliar was the constant use of strange farming terms. These had a particular fascination, though, for one whose father had been so interested in north-country dialect. Tasks like 'leading' oats, 'making mows', 'ligging hedges' and 'snaring turnips' were to be done, while 'gist' sheep and cattle were given 'eatage' for a few weeks in the process of 'agistment'. But although life was totally different from everything that he had previously known, and shorn of many of its cultural enjoyments, there was an overriding compensation: 'As we went out each morning to the labour of the fields there was always a feeling of satisfaction in knowing that in a world of death and destruction all our energies were devoted to the maintenance of life and health.'

This euphoria was temporarily shattered at the end of November when the War Agricultural Committee decided that, as there was not enough work for three men at Heanings during the winter months, John must now look elsewhere for employment. His reaction to the news was mixed: on the one hand there was a feeling of relief from what he called 'the servitude of taking orders', but on the other there was a genuine regret at leaving newly made friends, along with a sense of failure. 'My conscience would never have allowed me to run away from the land, but to be told to go was a very different matter,' he wrote. The prospect of finding a new employer was daunting, whereas the temptation to return home to his books was strong. He was able, however, to help with the move to Amherst Road and to do some more of his own writing.

New Year 1943 saw him start work on a farm at Kettlewell in upper Wharfedale, already a familiar area from childhood days. The family cottage had been at Hawkswick in nearby Littondale and the Moormans used to do their shopping at the village shop in Kettlewell that was still run by the same people. Apart from the searing memory of his father's drowning 24 years before, some of John's happiest days had been spent botanizing and bird-watching in those limestone dales. This fresh start as a farm-hand had, therefore, none of the mixture of novelty and uncertainty of his first venture; rather, it was a return to familiar territory and to work of which he had experience. Moreover, the farmhouse was in the heart of the village, which meant that he met many other people as he went by foot or bicycle to the scattered fields.

The work itself, however, could not have been more different. Heanings had been a 'ploughing farm' with practically no stock, whereas Kettlewell was a stock-farm with only three acres of ploughing. Consequently the hours of work were longer and the timetable each day unvaried. Starting at 6 am to clean out the 'shippens' before milking, the routine had to be carried out on Sundays as well, so the weekend was reduced to a few hours' free time between about 11 and 3 that day. 'The care of animals is the most exacting job in the world,' he reflected, 'comparable only with the care of little children.' Moreover, John was amazed to discover how well such a farmer knows his sheep, not merely distinguishing his own from those belonging to others, but also telling one sheep from another: 'This grey woolly sea in which we were standing knee-deep was not to him just a flock of sheep but a number of individual creatures whom he knew personally.' John compared this intimate knowledge of the shepherd with his own familiarity with the 4000 or so books from his own library, which he could identify by size or position on the shelf without looking at the title or author's name. Above all, the sketch of the Good Shepherd in John X now had greater depth as he delighted to hear an old shepherd of the dales counting his sheep in Gaelic numerals: 'ain, tain, tethera, methera, pimp, awfus, dawfus, deefus, dumpus, dick'.

Then there were new skills to be learned: 'gap-walling', or repairing the dry stone walls which were such a feature of the district; and scythe-sharpening, without which any attempt at mowing is useless. The popular view of work on the land being so simple that anyone could do it was quickly dispelled as John realized that the farmer and his men must be highly skilled craftsmen, responsible and intelligent. It took him all his time and energy to be 'even reasonably efficient'. Lady Day 1943 brought an unexpected shock, however, as John was told that he was to be replaced with a 'skilled' young man from college. By good fortune, Sep Close, who farmed at Scarr House at Buckden, further up the dale, took him on, and so began the longest and happiest stretch of John's time on the land, lasting more than twelve months until May of the following year. 'For Sep I soon developed a deep affection, enjoying and admiring his unfailing serenity and good humour,' he wrote; while for Sep's wife he had the greatest admiration: 'There was practically nothing she could not do', both in the house and on the farm.

Scarr House itself lay in the furthest stretch of the dale known as Langstrath, with its sonorously named hamlets of Hubberholme, Yockenthwaite, Beckermonds and Oughtershaw. John reckoned that little had changed there since Chaucer's time and liked to think that the two northern scholars of Soleres Hall who appear in the Reeve's Tale came from there-abouts. For example, those two lads regularly used 'I is' for 'I am', as is typical of that part of Craven, where 'wark' is still used for ache, 'capul' for horse and 'laithe' for barn. Further interest lay in the fact that Scarr House had been visited several times by George Fox and became an early centre of Quakerism in the dale; alongside it is a small plot of ground carefully walled in and bearing the inscription 'Friends Burial Ground 1650'. Two years later than that, Fox recorded in his diary, 'As I travelled through the dales I came to a man's house whose name was Tennant. I was moved to speak to the family and declare God's everlasting truth to them... He was convinced and his family and lived and died in the truth.' Twenty-five years later he wrote to his wife of 'a very large meeting' there. So John often thought of those former occupants,

> God-fearing men, reading their Bibles, meeting for silent worship in the farm kitchen, tending the graves of their friends and relatives in the little cemetery... I think of these generations of Yorkshire yeoman farmers who lived and worked here and I see how little life has changed at a farm such as this... I feel as if I had stepped out of the twentieth century, with its endless problems and anxieties and disappointments, into some other age, quieter, happier, more settled, more dignified.

Simplicity was the order of the day at Scarr House, for there was no plumbing except a cold tap in the back-kitchen; no illumination except paraffin lamps and candles. It all appealed to John's Franciscan streak. He was able, however, to go each week for a bath at Hubberholme vicarage. The vicar, the Revd Wilfred Menzies, and his wife became very good friends to John, as they welcomed him into their home, often giving him supper on Sunday evenings after John had played the harmonium, and sometimes preached, at Evensong. Intelligent conversation and the opportunity of playing the piano made 'the Hub' a place of refreshment after a hard week's work on the farm. This began at that critical time of the year in early May, when the cows begin to 'go t'door' or pasture outside,

while the hogs returning from their 'agistment' were 'gowded'
and dipped before being taken up to the moor for the summer
months. The gelding of tup-lambs followed in early June – an
experience remote from that of 'anaemic-looking shepherds in
stained-glass windows, carrying fat lambs as still and as quiet
as a sleeping baby'. Clipping the flock took up the rest of the
month until hay-making – that most crucial of all the farming
year's work – started in early July. In 1943 that was actually
completed by the last day of the month, appropriately fulfilling
the opening lines of *The Ballad of the Battle of Otterburn*:

> It fell about the Lammas-time
> When moormen win their hay…

So John excitedly wrote to Mary:

> Finished! at last! We have put the last forkful of hay in this
> afternoon about 2.30, so there is at last a moment to turn
> round and think again… During these last sixteen days we
> have practically never stopped. I wrote a few letters last
> Sunday morning, but otherwise have done nothing – neither
> letters, nor diary, nor reading, nor anything. I literally have
> not opened any book (except a hymnbook in church last
> Sunday) during these days!

Other letters to Mary from those days show that he was keeping a keen eye on the progress of the war. Italy was collapsing
and 'this big Russian drive might be the beginning of the end'.
But he was incensed that when the assassination of King Boris
of Bulgaria was announced on the radio, there was the added
comment, 'The wages of sin is death.' 'What blasphemy!' he
expostulated. 'Is it sin to go to war against, instead of for the
Allies?' Moreover, the twenty-fourth anniversary of his
father's death that September made him reflect on what it is to
lose a parent: 'When one of the wireless announcers remarks
casually that so many Germans have been killed I always think
of their families and what that will mean.' Four days later he
writes of his despair over the Church of England:

Nothing you can say can ever express one tenth of its badness... Twice in my lifetime it has been given a chance of choosing between a Gospel of sacrifice and love and a message of destruction and force – each time it has chosen the latter. I had great hopes (a) at the beginning of the war when Temple and Bell seemed so courageous and sensible, and (b) when we got rid of Cosmo [Lang], but we seem now to be going more and more downhill. Yet there is good work being done in a quiet way. It is the *official* side of the Church that it is so bad...

Such reflections about the progress of the war and the state of the Church were indicative really of John's readiness to get back to pastoral work and his books. His boyish pride in his achievements on the farm were nevertheless unabated, as for instance in April 1944 when setting potatoes: 'I came into my own as never before... I could put them in just *three* times as quick as Sep. If we set off side by side at the beginning of a row I used to meet him just halfway across as I was coming back!' And on another occasion he noted, 'Muck-spreading all day. I did 152 heaps which must be almost a record...' It needs to be remembered also that he weighed only seven-and-a-half stone and not surprisingly found the lifting of heavy weights one of the most difficult aspects of farm work. Moreover, medical opinion was that he should not have lifted anything heavier than himself. 'But,' as he said, 'no one could work on a farm and avoid lifting hundredweight bags. One afternoon I carried fifty of them, one after another, across our cow-yard.' Farm work was hard and the hours were long, but it was varied, and that made it more possible to carry on. In the same way, John would later reflect, a conscientious parish priest who puts in 65 to 70 hours a week finds that the constant variety of the work makes it absorbing rather than utterly exhausting.

At Michaelmas 1943, fire had burned down the barn and the hay which would have been winter feed for the cattle was destroyed. The beasts were therefore sold and there was less work to do. Was John justified in staying any longer? He went home for several weeks to read the proofs of *Church Life in England in the Thirteenth Century* and to get on with some other reading. Returning to Scarr House in January 1944 after three months away he confessed, 'To change suddenly from a life of literature to one of mucking-out is rather grim... But I often think of St Paul working with his hands. I hope he would have understood what I am trying to do.' Moreover, he was vastly amused to think that while he was mucking out he had a letter in his pocket from the Vice Chancellor of Cambridge University inviting him to preach the University sermon on 15 October. 'I felt like St Bonaventura who was planting cabbages when they brought him the Cardinal's hat, and who told them to hang it on the bush as he was busy.' But although he continued to work for Sep until May, John's mind was now definitely turned to thoughts of an active ministry again, or even an academic post. Professor F. M. Powicke had confided in Professor A. J. Grant that John might perhaps be considered for the Dixie Professorship of Ecclesiastical History at Cambridge, carrying with it a Fellowship at his old college, Emmanuel. There was a possibility that a small theological college for eight or nine students might be set up at Whittlesford, near Cambridge, and John went to see Professor Charles Raven about it; and William Temple had him to lunch at Lambeth and asked about his books and after Mary as well. But most of all his mind dwelt on the possibility of a country parish where both of them could 'write a few books now and then and I could help milk the cows for farmers when they were off sick'. He speculated that it would be 'nice' – a favourite adjective of his – to be in Cumbria near his friends the du Toits and the Croppers: 'It would be better than flying after teaching jobs and that sort of thing.' Above all, he was quite clear in his mind that he did not want another Manchester parish or 'one of those Lancashire cotton towns'.

He also hankered, though, after training ordinands and with that in mind lunched with Bishop Leslie Owen of Maidstone, who told him that 3000 men had 'given in their names' for training when the war was ended. But he doubted whether

CACTM (the Central Advisory Council for the Ministry) really had a plan to enable this and felt that Owen himself lacked the drive to set things up. When he went up to Cambridge to deliver his University sermon he saw Greer and Abbott at Westcott House, but felt that they were part of 'a small clique, jealous of outsiders and not wanting rivals to older-established colleges'.[4] At the same time now he was depressed by the fact that although Bishop Guy Warman had written some months earlier expressing his anxiety about John and his willingness to help him find a parish – 'these things take a little time,' he said – nevertheless five northern bishops to whom he had written did not seem to be finding him a suitable country parish. The Bishop of Coventry, however, expressed his willingness to put John's name forward to a private patron for a parish of some 150 souls. But this would have been 'too comfy', he felt.

His depression was deepened by the news of the death in October 1944 of William Temple, which he regarded as 'a disaster of the greatest magnitude'. He was 'the one really great man whom we have got – great in every possible way'. It was at this juncture that Lord Carlisle restored his confidence by offering him Lanercost.

## Notes

1. See letter in *Theology*, 42.251, (May 1941), pp. 300–2.
2. Alan Wilkinson: *Dissent or Conform? War and Peace and the English Churches, 1900–1945* (SCM Press, 1986), p. 291.
3. Anna Maria Phillips, aunt of George Macaulay Trevelyan and daughter of the Liberal MP for Bury.
4. William Greer was then Principal of Westcott, whilst Eric Abbott was Warden of Lincoln Theological College.

# Lanercost and Chichester:
# Training Men for the Ministry

Lanercost was to be a turning-point for John and Mary, providing the ideal place to re-establish their partnership after wartime separation, as well as a parochial context where both could pursue their scholarly interests in a congenial, rural setting. Situated twelve miles north-east of Carlisle on the River Irthing, and close to the Roman Wall, the parish covered a large area consisting of isolated farms and cottages. At its heart was the Priory, founded in 1166 by Augustinian canons and completed in 1220. 'Vast, lofty and bleak', is how John described it, with a similarly bare interior which had 'no colour, nor cross and candles'. John's feeling that it was very much in the Evangelical tradition was confirmed when he met the previous incumbent: 'the opposite of me in every way'. The adjacent Elizabethan stone rectory incorporated the thirteenth-century guest-house of the Priory, where King Edward I and Queen Eleanor had stayed on several occasions, the last being for a ruinous 22 weeks during the King's illness in the winter of 1306 – 1307. Mainly north-facing, this rectory was equally forbidding, but John and Mary had no hesitation in accepting the offer of the living and moved there in February 1945.

John immediately bought a brass cross for the church and Mary had spent £1 in Carlisle on two bunches of daffodils for the institution and induction:

We had put these on the altar – they have never had flowers before – and they made the east end look quite lovely. The

sun came out during the service and lit up the old red sand-
stone of the ruins, which can be seen through the east
window. The whole effect was moving.

Warmth and colour were also brought through daily worship
and the administration of all but one of the seven sacraments
in the course of the ensuing 18 months. The history of the
Priory fascinated John; he wrote a model and well-researched
guide-book for visitors, as well as a paper for the *English
Historical Review* entitled 'Edward I at Lanercost'.[1] But his
main writing here was *B. K. Cunningham: A Memoir*, at the
invitation of a small group consisting of Bishop Wynn of Ely,
Eric Abbott, then Dean of King's College, London, and
William Greer, B.K.'s successor as Principal of Westcott
House. Unexpected as this was, John accepted it with alacrity,
feeling that he would learn much from it and he enjoyed being
in touch with many friends in the process. At the same time, in
March 1945, he was gratified to learn that Cambridge
University had awarded him a Doctorate of Divinity for his
book *Church Life in England in the Thirteenth Century*. The
University Press published it in June and its 15,000 copies
were sold out within six weeks. John's aim in this work was to
produce what he called 'a snap-shot' of the century which lay
'at the centre of what, for this country, may be regarded as the
great medieval period' rather than 'a film' of the Middle Ages
as a whole. It was 'a century of great men and of a great
experiment', for in the single generation when Robert
Grosseteste was at Lincoln (1235 – 53) there were eight other
'first class men'[2] all labouring for reform, supported by the
energy and heroism of the early Franciscans and Dominicans.
Although their zeal disappointingly did not bring about
greater reforms in Church life, John could not fail to take
courage from their example, and this undoubtedly inspired
him in his own episcopal work later. The sad rivalry and
jealousy between the two Mendicant Orders and their lack of
co-operation with the parochial clergy meant that a great
opportunity for reform in the Church had been lost, which

might otherwise, he wrote, have made unnecessary 'the disastrous turmoil of the 16th century'. Reviews of the book were generally favourable, though F. M. Powicke,[3] who had been alarmed at John's absence from libraries while working on the land, felt that it was not as good as his work on the Franciscan sources, which had gained him the degree of Bachelor of Divinity. Other scholars pointed to various omissions: 'the great devotional movement from Anselm to Pecham' (Raby), 'the creative ideas and ideals of the medieval world' in scholastic theology, religious art and architecture (Knowles), and, typical of Coulton, 'the fear of hell, intolerance and clerical concubinage'. All, however, applauded its sweep and readability, as well as agreeing with its main conclusions.

Apart from the pastoral care of his scattered flock, the most important part of John's work at Lanercost was in training three mature men for ordination. Two had been schoolmasters and one a businessman; they came to the rectory one day each week for tuition and prayer. 'I have almost got my college!' John wrote. The morning would be devoted to lectures on the Old and New Testaments, with Doctrine and Worship in the afternoon. Vast subjects could only be outlined as they strove to get through a two-year course in six months. The day would then end with Evensong and devotional address. This happy and disciplined routine, however, was soon to be shattered when in March 1946 John received a letter from the Bishop of Chichester, George Bell, inviting him to become Principal of Chichester Theological College which was to be reopened after its wartime evacuation first to Cambridge and then to Edinburgh. 'I realise that you are much wedded to the North,' Bell wrote, adding 'Greer put forward your name,' and 'I am very anxious that Chichester should specialize in training for country parishes.'

Chichester was one of the oldest of Anglican theological colleges: founded in 1839, 11 years after Queen's College, Birmingham, and continuing until it was 'axed' by the House of Bishops in 1994. It was the first to be sited in a cathedral city where the resources of scholarship and tradition could be drawn upon. In particular its Tractarian origin and ethos made a strong appeal to John. But, 'It is too soon to be moving', was his immediate reaction. More than that, 'Mary is very much against my going – as I am in my heart'. Life at Lanercost was good for them both and John had various projects for books which probably could not be furthered in the busy life of teaching, administration and ministerial training at Chichester. Moreover, it would mean moving to the south, far from their beloved north where they both had their roots. The College 'used to be a very spiky place', John commented; though Bishop Bell reassured him that he wanted to 'bring it down to a more central position'.

After a week, then, John wrote to Bell to decline the offer. Straightaway, however, he felt unhappy about it: had he turned it down for the wrong reason? Would he have gone if he had been single? But 'there was no possibility of making a success of the job if Mary was going to be miserable there'. Then again he had to admit that Lanercost was not entirely satisfying, and of the two jobs it could more easily be done by someone else. 'I want to get my teeth into a job which will demand all that I have to give. I love teaching and have always felt drawn towards training men for the ministry. If the powers-that-be think that I can do it, ought I to refuse?' The prospect, too, of working close to George Bell, whose stand against the mass-bombing of German towns he had so much admired, must have appealed to him, just as John's own wartime protest had interested Bell. So at the end of March John wrote again to Bell, suggesting that he should at least go down to Chichester to talk with him about it. Several weeks of further doubt and discussion with Mary followed, but when on 7 June the College Council unanimously agreed to offer him the Principalship, with which Bell signified that he intended to combine the Chancellorship of the Cathedral, John finally accepted.

Thus after only 18 months at Lanercost, John moved – on his own at first – to Chichester in September 1946, and the College reopened its doors on 21 October. To reduce its debts,

however, the main buildings on the north side of Westgate had
been sold and an attractive Georgian red-brick house on the
south side of the street now became the main college building.
It was named Marriott House after the first Principal, Charles
Marriott of Oriel, and further accommodation was made
available in the Bishop's Palace. The medieval chapel at the
Palace, with its memories of St Richard and its beautiful
thirteenth-century roundel of the Virgin and Child, was generously shared by the Bishop with the College for its daily round
of offices and Eucharist. Bell's own participation in worship
with the students from time to time was an added inspiration.
Alongside this a strong link with the Cathedral was established, enabling much to be learned from the dignified order-
ing of worship according to 'the English Use'⁴ which Dean
Duncan-Jones had established there. 'In the old days,' John
wrote in his diary, 'the College regarded the Cathedral with
great suspicion and there was little contact between the two.
The students mostly attended St Bart's, the most extreme
Anglo-Catholic church in the town. But now we all attend
Evensong in the Cathedral on Wednesdays and Saturdays and
most of us go there on Sunday... I like having this association
with the Cathedral as Chancellor and I very much enjoy the
services. Hawkins, the Organist, is a delightful and brilliant
man and there is a good spirit in the choir.' Hawkins, who had
trained in Paris under Widor, became a good friend of the
College and helped the students with their singing of the office
and plainsong. Intelligent use of the *Book of Common Prayer*
characterized the worship of both Cathedral and College. Max
Godden, who had served in the RAF before going up to
Oxford and then becoming a student at the College in 1950,
wrote: 'What I learnt was a true and steady Anglicanism and I
think I am just beginning to understand what a wonderful and
solid thing it is.' Max eventually became Archdeacon of Lewes
and Hastings, and John sometimes stayed with him at Glynde
rectory when he had to come south for meetings in later years.

John himself lectured on Church History, Worship
and Pastoralia, while Richard Cole, the Vice-Principal, was

responsible for New Testament and Doctrine. Canon
Lowther-Clarke from the Cathedral, and the Revd Richard
Ratcliff, Vicar of St George's, Whyke, were enlisted as
'honorary tutors', being responsible for the Old Testament and
Ethics respectively. A year later the Revd Cyril Adams joined
the staff, quite soon becoming Vice-Principal with the Revd
James Hannon appointed as Chaplain in July 1949, by which
time student numbers had increased significantly. There had
been nine students at the outset: two had served in the RNVR
and three had been in the Army, while Brother Peter OSP was
a monk from Alton Abbey. Commander Eric Staples recalls
how he arrived at the beginning of October, three weeks
before term was due to begin, to help get the house ready after
its wartime occupation by the Army. Then followed the hard
work of clearing 80 tons of rubble which had been used to
make a car-park and so to recover the lawn. Brother Peter also
recalls that the roof of the College leaked and he had to cover
his bed with brown paper at night until it was repaired. It was
a pioneering situation, with Spartan conditions but much happiness. Many of these first students, as well as later ones,
became firm friends with whom John kept in touch until the
end of his life. Four married men were soon allowed to live in
the town with their wives: this was a considerable innovation
at a time when most theological colleges were still very monas-
tic in ethos. An early visitor to the College was Pastor Martin
Niemöller, whose anti-Nazi activities had led to his being put
in a concentration camp during the war. He and his wife came
to Chichester as guests of Bishop and Mrs Bell, returning in
1949 for the first meeting of the Central Committee of the
World Council of Churches. John wrote that his visit was
'almost like having St Polycarp or one of the other martyrs'.

Once again, just as John had stabilized a situation, a tempt-
ing invitation was presented to him. In August 1947 William
Greer was elevated to the See of Manchester and John was
asked by the Governors of Westcott House to succeed him as
Principal. He records that he turned down the offer 'not without considerable regret'. In talking to his father-in-law about

it, he had let slip the comment that perhaps it would not be 'a very Christian thing' to accept. Trevelyan, who as Master of Trinity would naturally have welcomed having John and Mary in Cambridge, rejoined, 'I don't know about your Christianity, but it would be a damned ungentlemanly thing to do.' So John remained at Chichester, encouraged by the report of the Bishops' inspectors in July 1949: 'We conclude our Report by emphasising the impression of sanity and proportion made upon us by the atmosphere and tone of the College... "Detached" colleges used to be criticised as hothouses of intro-verted and pietistic ecclesiasticism: we doubt whether any College can be less open to such a charge than the Chichester of today.' It was a vindication of John's policy of not running a seminary and also ensuring that there was always a broad mix of age, churchmanship and academic background among the students. The walk along West Street from dining and lecture rooms to services in chapel, taken three or four times daily, meant going out into the open air and encountering townspeople on their daily business. This earthed them in the wider community and the world as it actually is. But John was very severe with two of the students who went to have mid-morning coffee in the town. 'Widows have given their mites to enable you to study here,' he told them.

By August 1950, when Clement Attlee offered John the deanery of Ely, which he had no hesitation in turning down, the College had reached its highest number of 39 students, nine of whom were married. With an early start as well as a late end to the day in the chapel, the afternoons were left free for walks, gardening and the maintenance of the sports field. Annual hockey and cricket matches against Salisbury Theological College were played, at which both Principals 'bullied off' and were key batsmen. One year at hockey John broke his collar-bone; then memorably at Stansted Park in the year of the Queen's coronation (1953), the Salisbury wickets tumbled at the sight of the Earl of Bessborough bringing Queen Salote of Tonga on to the field to watch.

Mary, although she was busy writing her biography of

William Wordsworth,[5] at first found it difficult to integrate
into the life of the College, being the first wife of one of its
Principals in living memory. She found a role, however, in
teaching New Testament Greek, in supervising the gardening
team and in holding occasional literary evenings in the flat.
George Bell would also come to read some of his favourite
poetry – Browning, Hopkins, Eliot and Betjeman. Two
memorable dramatic productions were put on by the students:
*The Price of a Slave*, written by two of them, Patrick
Appleford and Philip Turner, in Passiontide 1951 and *Love's
Labour's Lost*, performed in the open air in May 1952. Mary's
encouragement of all this was only surpassed by her excitement when a hoopoe, rarely seen in England, strutted across
the lawn, delaying supper while the bird lingered. She had
waited 30 years for this sight. Next morning a realistic mock-
up of the bird, complete with variegated plumage and crest
was there to greet the bleary-eyed as they came into breakfast.
John found it difficult not to smile, typically biting his lower
lip and slightly raising his eyebrows, while Mary in her turn
exploded with laughter – eventually.

Together they took a few students to Rome and Assisi in the
early 1950s, and when there in 1952 John lectured in Italian
on 'The Study of St Francis in England' at Franciscan houses
in both places. On one of these occasions the party marvelled
to see two aged Franciscan bishops go forward and kiss his
hand, looking for an episcopal ring which was not yet there.
Later in life he would enjoy being teased about this incident,
which betrayed his own vanity. Because of this honest assessment of himself John was able to deliver to different
generations of students a series of addresses at Compline on
the names of the clergy – minister, pastor, priest, and so on.
Expectations mounted as he reached 'father', and were
rewarded by his memorable words, 'Too many clergy put off
the old man only to put on the old woman'. In another address
he told the students that one of their greatest privileges would
be to read the Scriptures to their people, and that they should
not allow anyone else to do so without proper rehearsal. As

Chancellor of the Cathedral he gave a prize each year to the best reader among the boys at the Prebendal School, being vastly amused when one of them spoke of the Prodigal Son wasting his substance with 'ree-o-tus' living.

Three of John's students from the early 1950s later became bishops: Morris Maddocks (Selby, 1972), Michael Manktelow (Basingstoke, 1977) and Christopher Luxmoore (Bermuda, 1984). It was also at the height of his time at Chichester that John's best-known book, *A History of the Church in England* (1953) was published. Almost 60 years had passed since Wakeman's one-volume history appeared in 1896, and although that had been revised by S. L. Ollard some 20 years later, there was now what Professor Norman Sykes called 'a clamant need' for a new volume. John himself recognized that his attempt 'to compress the history of 1750 years into 400 pages' could be 'no more than an introduction', for he traced the beginnings of *Ecclesia Anglicana* to the bringing of the Gospel to England at least by the year 200, some four centuries before Augustine was sent from Rome. Sykes commented that its 'outstanding merit is its comprehensiveness of scope'. Others commended its clarity, its balanced judgements and its readability. His father-in-law was delighted that learning was not developed at the expense of writing and saw it as complementing his own immensely popular *English Social History*, while his bishop marvelled that he had been able to achieve such a book in the midst of his other labours.

Undoubtedly John's experience in lecturing for the General Ordination Exam on English Church History had ordered a wealth of material in his mind and made it easier to assimilate. His clear presentation disguised a vast amount of knowledge and wide reading, while in its attempt to be accurate the book avoided the dullness of being impartial. John did not shrink from making his own assessments of major figures like Thomas Becket and King Charles I. The former was 'One of those men who visualise the part they are to play and then adapt their lives to the type they have created in their own minds', while the latter he deemed exasperating, duplicitous and irresponsible, not to be romanticized as a martyr just because he was beheaded. Nevertheless, he comments, 'So Charles died, but with his death the fate of Puritanism was sealed and the Church's future ensured'. Former pupils rejoiced to see the sentence which always raised a laugh in John's lectures about Henry VIII's first wife: 'Now Katharine was Charles's [i.e. Charley's] aunt.' *The Times Educational Supplement* perhaps best summed it up as 'That rare achievement, sufficiently biased as a piece of authentic historical writing in which the author communicates his interest to the reader without misleading him.' Indeed so successful was this book that it reached a third edition 20 years later, with the addition of a new final chapter bringing it up to the 1970s. Minor alterations were made in 1985 and it has not been superseded as a one-volume history book nearly 50 years after its original publication. Its important contribution to an understanding of Anglicanism for a vast number of readers all over the world must rank highly in the list of John's achievements, not least at Chichester.

'It was a great time to be at Chichester with Bell, Duncan-Jones and Lowther-Clarke,' John reminisced to one of his students towards the end of his life. His admiration for George Bell was unqualified: here was 'a truly catholic bishop', known the world over for his courage in denouncing the war-time bombing policy which led to the loss of innocent civilian lives, for his support of those within Germany who were working for the overthrow of Hitler, and for his unstinting determination to bring the World Council of Churches into being. Later in life John was particularly proud to wear George's episcopal ring, not least during his own ecumenical work, feeling that he was carrying on in the same independent, yet essentially Anglican, spirit.

John was not always, however, a very comfortable member of the Administrative Chapter of the Cathedral and at one time wondered whether he could give up his seat on it. He felt, though, that he could not do so 'without causing a lot of bother and suspicion'. Bishop Bell had conducted his Primary

Visitation in 1948 and in his Charge of 4 November clarified the responsibilities of the dignitaries of the Cathedral. The Chapter was dominated by A. S. Duncan-Jones, the Dean, who had pioneered the liturgical Customary of the Cathedral in faithful adherence to the 1928 Prayer Book and the ideals of the Alcuin Club. Impressive in stature, wearing his grey cassock, with gown, bands and Canterbury cap, he was forceful in his rebuke of John who had turned up to his first Chapter meeting in a sports-jacket. For his part John was horrified at the trivial business which engaged such dignitaries in Chapter, not least the discussion as to what was the appropriate rent to be charged for a fish and chip shop on Cathedral property. Nevertheless he penned a suitable apology in Latin for the Dean, sending it round by hand of a Benedictine monk. The Precentor, A. R. Browne-Wilkinson, was an acknowledged authority on religious education and children's work, whom John had known as a parish priest in Wensleydale. The Bursalis Prebendary was W. K. Lowther-Clarke, whose learning and sanctity made him a living example of that *stupor mundi* which had in an earlier century been applied to Anglican clergy as a whole. The Treasurer, C. B. Mortlock, was largely absentee as he held a benefice in the City of London where his main ministry was as a particularly urbane ecclesiastical journalist.

The Archdeacon of Chichester was Lancelot Mason, with whom John had partly overlapped at Westcott House in the late 1920s. His somewhat rigid personality did not make for the easiest relationship, and this was to come to a head with their open disagreement in assessing the archiepiscopate of Randall Davidson. In an article for *Theology* (July 1956), John reviewed the quality of Davidson's leadership some 25 years after his death. For one who had been brought up as a Presbyterian, his rise to the highest office in the Church of England had been 'rapid and startling'. John saw him as essentially cautious and negative rather than visionary and inspirational, with a view of the Church as 'a great institution for the moral improvement of the people of England'.[6] He was particularly critical of Davidson's Charge to the Diocese of Canterbury (1912) which failed to mention 'how the Church originated or what place it holds in the teaching of Christ and the apostles, or what part it must play in the divine economy'. He had not dwelt on its worship, its purveyance of Grace through Word and Sacrament, nor even of its having a Gospel to proclaim.

Mason, who had been brought up in the Close at Canterbury where his father was a Canon, not only knew Davidson but had also been Bell's chaplain when the latter was writing his monumental *Life* of Davidson. So he wrote a vehement letter to the Editor of *Theology*,[7] objecting to John's 'strangely distorted portrait' and questioning his methods. Above all, he claimed that Davidson had deliberately limited his scope in the Charge of 1912 and that John had not taken into account his earlier Charges in the Dioceses of Rochester and Winchester. 'These omissions raise the question whether Dr. Moorman has properly examined the evidence before reaching his verdict.' John's rejoinder, after a careful study of those earlier Charges, was that there was no need to alter his thesis. 'To any independent historian,' he concluded, 'looking back on the recent history of the Church, there can be no doubt that, during the first quarter of this century, the Anglican Church in this country lost a great deal of ground. The question is bound to be asked sooner or later: "What sort of leadership was the Church getting during those critical years?"; or more specifically, "Was Randall Davidson qualified to give the right sort of lead?" It is too early as yet to answer these questions; but after a fairly close study of his Charges, letters, and other printed works, one is left in considerable doubt.'

Canon Charles Smyth, then Rector of St Margaret's Westminster, who relished an academic fight as well as a tilt at the Establishment, wrote quickly to congratulate John on his 'masterly article' on 'this great man with great limitations'. Smyth would also have been present when John had delivered the Gore Memorial Lecture in Westminster Abbey that year.

Taking as his theme 'Charles Gore and the Doctrine of the Church',[8] John showed how, by both his teaching and his practice, Gore had developed the Tractarians' emphasis upon the Apostolic Succession and the concept of a Visible Church, particularly in his *The Church and the Ministry*.[9] Emphasizing that the Church of Christ was more than a national institution or 'a man-made society for mutual support and moral progress', he proclaimed it as 'the extension of the Incarnation' demanding both a Visible Church and Sacramental Worship. Thus, when the Enabling Act, providing for lay representation in the new Church Assembly, was passed in 1919 Gore was distressed that Baptism rather than Confirmation was taken as the necessary qualification for the franchise. Feeling that this flew in the face of all his teaching, he resigned from the See of Oxford. Davidson with his different view of the Church might have won the day on this issue, but as John insisted, 'Gore did not fail. It is true that he failed to carry the Church with him on this point; but in other ways his influence was deep and lasting.' It could equally have been said of John himself in his own episcopate and ecumenical work.

Smyth also wrote, 'I am so sorry you are leaving Chichester: you have done very notable work there and you will not be easy to replace.' It was a timely recognition by the wider Church of John's re-creation of Chichester Theological College, as significant in every way as its original foundation. But John felt that after ten years as Principal the College would now profit from new blood and new ideas: moreover, he wanted more time to work on his major work, *A History of the Franciscan Order*. Therefore, early in 1956 he announced his intention to resign at the end of September and retreat to the Lake District. He had hoped that he might continue to hold the office of Chancellor of the Cathedral, pointing to the example of C.B. Mortlock as non-resident Treasurer, but George Bell was adamant that the office should continue to be linked with that of Principal of the Theological College. In the event, John was delighted that Canon Cheslyn Jones was appointed as his successor in both offices, and that under his leadership the number of students rose into the fifties with five members of staff. John himself was collated to the prebendal stall of Heathfield when it fell vacant that autumn, and ironically it was Lancelot Mason who, as Canon in Residence, presented him with a copy of the Authorized Version at his installation.

The Moormans' departure from Chichester was inevitably demanding, both physically and emotionally. The offer of a canonry at Windsor to succeed Alec Vidler in the training of older men for ordination was something which John had no hesitation in turning down. It would have been like going 'out of the frying-pan and into the fire', he wrote; he wanted un-interrupted time in which to write. But while he was packing his books to leave Chichester for Longsleddale, on the very day when the farewell party for him and Mary was to be held in the College, 7 September 1956, there were tragic develop-ments which made even greater demands on their emotional reserves. That morning as John came in from chapel, Mary handed him the telephone, saying, 'It's Theo. Your mother has had a very bad heart attack during the night. And *mine* has died.' Next morning came the news that Frances had now died, poignantly on the thirty-seventh anniversary of her husband's death. 'What a wonderful mother she has been, and how much I owe to her,' John wrote that day in his diary. She was within a month of her eighty-ninth birthday, she had not seen a doctor for over three years, and her last years in Leeds had been very full and happy. 'She is my oldest friend and no one can ever fill the place she held in our lives.' They had writ-ten to each other at least two or three times every week and Frances had always addressed her son as 'darling Jonathan'.

With two family funerals now to follow in the next week, John had to withdraw from leading a small group of Anglican priests who had been invited to stay in Milan with Archbishop Montini. The previous year Montini had been visited by George Bell, and 'each took an immediate liking to the other'.[10] Bell observed that Montini was 'like a curate being discreetly critical of his Vicar' (i.e. the Pope) who had often urged collaboration with 'the separated brethren' without saying how this might be done.[11] Doubtless Bell was party to the issuing of this invitation to the group which now included the Revds Bernard Pawley, C. L. Gage-Brown, John Dickinson and Colin James, who were joined by Colin Hickling, then still a student at the College and an Italian speaker.[12] Despite not being able to journey with the group at that time, John was within the decade able to form a deep friendship with Montini, which spilled over into the vastly improved relations between their two great Churches (see Chapter 7).

## Notes

1. *English Historical Review* 67 (1952), pp. 161–74.
2. Namely, Edmund Rich, Richard of Chichester, Hugh Northwold, Alexander Stavensby, Walter Cantilupe, Ralph Maidstone, Walter Gray and Richard le Poore.
3. Regius Professor of Modern History at Oxford University, 1928–47.
4. See *The Chichester Customary* (SPCK, 1948).
5. *William Wordsworth: A Biography* (2 vols; Oxford University Press, 1957–65).
6. *Theology*, 59. 433, (July 1956), pp. 269–75.
7. *Theology*, 59. 435, (September 1956), pp. 377–9.
8. See *Church Quarterly Review* (April–June 1957).
9. 1888; rev. edn by C. H. Turner, 1919. Longmans, Green.
10. B. Pawley and M. Pawley, *Rome and Canterbury through Four Centuries* (Mowbrays, 1974), p. 327.
11. R. C. D. Jasper, *George Bell, Bishop of Chichester* (Oxford University Press, 1967), p. 337.
12. See also Peter Hebblethwaite, *Paul VI: The First Modern Pope* (Harper Collins, 1993), pp. 267–70.

# 5

# Franciscan Scholar

Eight of John Moorman's fifteen books are about St Francis and his teaching, and the development of the Franciscan Order in the medieval period. These books were flanked by his first and last printed articles: – the former in *Theology* (October 1929) on 'The Permanent Element in the Life and Teaching of St Francis', and the latter his contribution on 'Franciscan Spirituality' for The Study of Spirituality in 1986.[1] All had been written and researched during his active ministry as parish priest, theological college principal and diocesan bishop. At Chichester and later in Ripon he had facilitated this concentration by having two desks in his study, one for his current work and the other for his Franciscan studies, and he would move across to the latter whenever a spare half hour or so presented itself.

The early article had warned against a false picture of the saint as just the founder of an Order or as social reformer or even as critic of the Church. His one purpose had been 'to obey Christ', quite literally applying the dominical injunctions to himself. Thus Francis must not be seen as one to be slavishly imitated or as providing a panacea for today's problems, but rather as an inspiration to one's own self-surrender to that duty which Christ requires of each individual. 'I have done my duty, may Christ teach you yours', as Francis himself said when dying, pointing thus to the Lord and not the disciple. 'The more we study the life of St Francis the more we shall be enabled to understand his spirit of complete self-surrender.'[2]

John therefore set about studying the earliest accounts of the saint's life, grappling with their chronology in his first major work of scholarship, *The Sources for the Life of St Francis of Assisi*, published by Manchester University Press in 1940. With a foreword by Dr A. G. Little, then doyen of English Franciscan scholars, it earned him not only the degree of Bachelor of Divinity at Cambridge, but also the comment from Professor F. M. Powicke, 'Well, I think you've settled that hash all right'. The 'hash' referred to was the confusion resulting from Paul Sabatier's mistake over the date of *Tres Socii*, which that brilliant inaugurator of modern Franciscan studies had read as 1227 and not the actual 1318. Sabatier had been correct, however, in sensing that *Tres Socii* gave the real picture of Francis by his actual contemporaries – Leo, Angelo and Ruffino. Acknowledging 'the new lease of life' given to the study of the sources by his own mentor, F. C. Burkitt,[3] in 1926, John applied the principles of the higher criticism learned in his New Testament studies to compare the texts of *Celano I* and *Tres Socii*, showing the latter to be more primitive.

Leading scholars of the time voiced their approval of John's thesis, none more generously than F. M. Powicke,[4] who hailed it as 'the starting-point' for all future investigation. 'That is something like a review, coming from such a quarter,' wrote G. M. Trevelyan to John. 'To make a conquest of both Little and Powicke is a feat indeed. I felt when I read your book the kind of intellectual interest and consent that one only gives to something masterly, but the pleasure is very great to me that it is really *so*.' He added as an aside, 'I like to think of the one day a week digging: I am sure it is right and Franciscan, and it will keep you well.' Professor Margaret Deanesley was equally positive in *Theology*,[5] while Dom David Knowles confessed in a letter to John to being 'converted entirely' by the main thesis in what he called 'an extraordinarily satisfying book'. But on the Continent a time-bomb was ticking away, exploding some six years later. Remarkably in the difficult circumstances of war, when normal channels of communication were dislocated, a copy of *Sources* had reached the convent of Quaracchi, near Florence, apparently from Ireland. There the renowned German Franciscan scholar, Fr Michael Bihl OFM, wrote a severe and lengthy attack.[6] John was to address this in the preface to the reprint of *Sources* in 1966: he felt that Bihl's objection resulted both from a complete misunderstanding of his intention as well as from unfamiliarity with the critical methods that had long been used in biblical scholarship. John, therefore, contended that although much had been written on the early Franciscan literature in the 25 years that had ensued since its first publication, 'the main arguments of the book will stand up to reasonable criticism'.

In 1946 he produced *A New Fioretti*, 'a collection of early stories about St Francis of Assisi hitherto untranslated'. Portraying the saint as 'one of the greatest actors the world has ever known', here are assembled some 75 tales of dramatic incidents in the saint's life. Their effect was to redress the balance of the more formal *Lives* written by Celano and Bonaventura, and to emphasize Francis's ideas of simplicity and poverty, along with his mistrust of scholarship. Four years later John followed this up with his own *Life of St Francis*.[7] Making no apology for adding to the already immense literature on the subject, he wrote in not much more than 100 pages an account which is both scholarly and readable. After several reprints, a new edition was published in 1976 to mark the seven-hundred-and-fiftieth anniversary of the saint's death: it has more than stood the test of time. 'Francis,' he wrote, 'has undoubtedly a very special message to those of us who live in a highly materialistic world where money is so often regarded as the only criterion of contentment...' But he insists that 'The call of St Francis was not to escape from the world, but to give oneself to the world, asking for nothing for oneself and ready to suffer and to die for the souls of men'.

Two years later, in 1952, *The Grey Friars in Cambridge* appeared, being the substance of the Birbeck Lectures given under the auspices of Trinity College in 1948–49. Some 60 years earlier Dr A. G. Little had written about the Grey Friars in Oxford and often afterwards had urged his friends in Cambridge to produce a parallel volume. John had planned in his undergraduate days to take up the challenge, and, although

Little was sadly not to live to see the result, the invitation from Trinity provided the necessary spur to do so. It was an additional pleasure that John was able to stay with Mary's parents in Trinity Master's Lodge while delivering the lectures. More poignantly, however, he had to record in his final lecture that at the Dissolution ordered by Henry VIII large quantities of stone and timber from the friars' deserted building were used for the Great Court and Chapel of the new Trinity College, while the site of the friary was sold for the founding of Sidney Sussex College. An old wall in the garden there is the sole remain of the friary which had earlier contributed so much to Cambridge life and learning.

John's *magnum opus* in the field of Franciscan studies was, however, *A History of the Franciscan Order from its Origins to the Year 1517*. Largely the result of the three years he had spent in Longsleddale after relinquishing the Principalship of Chichester Theological College, in its original form it ran to 400,000 words, and perhaps for that reason was not accepted by Cambridge University Press which had previously published both his *Church Life in England in the Thirteenth Century* and *The Grey Friars in Cambridge*. So after he had gone to Ripon and was busily engaged in being a diocesan bishop, John worked to reduce its size, sending it to Oxford University Press in 1965.

'I have now done a great deal more work on this book,' he wrote, 'and have decided that my hope of producing what would be regarded as a standard work on the medieval Franciscans was perhaps more than I should have hoped for. I have, therefore, reduced this book to about 295,000 words, which makes it possible to print it as one volume... I have cut out a good deal of detail and have tried to produce a book which will be of general use to students of medieval history... There is no doubt a great need for a book of this kind. There is in fact no history of the medieval Franciscans in any language at the present time.'

Professor Margaret Deanesley of London University, who had read it in typescript, opined that 'it should be a classic, read for 200 years'. She feared, however, that more than the book's original length, 'the main difficulty is that medieval history is not taught in any of the new proliferating universities. And not as much in the two other universities as it ought to be.' Above all, though, she felt that it was 'A credit to the English bench of bishops to have produced it'.[8] Perhaps that is the work's greatest significance, in that it was completed and prepared for the press by a twentieth-century diocesan bishop while in office. Michael Ramsey had encouraged John to accept the See of Ripon on the understanding that the episcopal bench needed to include scholars who would still study and write books. Now he devoured his copy of John's work with delight and admiration. 'Some of it requires more intelligence than I have,' he wrote, 'but much of it is very much "up my street" and I expect to get very much enjoyment and profit out of it. I am very proud that a friend and colleague has produced such a work and that the dictum that "a mitre is an extinguisher" should in your case be so belied.' Dom David Knowles was similarly impressed by this fact, admiring the erudition and skill with which 'the daunting complexity and extent of the subject' had been tackled, but admitting to being left 'a little unsatisfied', feeling that the book was 'neither analytical nor critical', and also 'quite passionless'.[9] From Oxford itself Dr Marjorie Reeves[10] commended 'the directness and freshness' with which 'the narrative of a well-known story' had been written. Pointing, however, to 'the great theme of all Franciscan history: the conflicting interpretations of the meaning of poverty', she identified the omission of the apocalyptic dimension in the Spirituals' defence of extreme poverty, as well as the failure to assess the nature and power of Joachim of Fiore's influence over them. Then she commented, 'The scholarship unobtrusively displayed in footnotes and massively collected in the bibliography is prodigious. The synthesis of all this material is a work of art.'

*A History of the Franciscan Order* was eventually published in 1968 and went out of print 11 years later, but John lived to see it reprinted in 1988 by the Franciscan Herald Press in

Chicago.[11] After the success of the *magnum opus* two subsequent books were slighter, though significant, additions to the corpus of John's Franciscan writings: *The Franciscans in England* was published in 1974, with a preface by Cardinal Heenan,[12] and *Richest of Poor Men* three years later.[13] The former was written to mark the seven-hundred-and-fiftieth anniversary of the arrival of the friars at Dover on 10 September 1224 – within the actual lifetime of St Francis. From small beginnings in Canterbury they had quickly spread to London, Oxford and Cambridge, until by the end of the thirteenth century there were 59 houses all over the country. John estimated that 300 years after their arrival there were about 1000 Franciscans in England, but it looked as if the Franciscan movement here had come to an end soon afterwards with the dissolution of the friaries and dispersal of their occupants. The tradition was maintained, however, by Franciscan missionaries from the Continent. Later the flowering of interest in St Francis towards the end of the nineteenth century led to the beginnings of an 'active, professed Anglican Franciscan movement' with James Adderley, Vicar of Plaistow. Remarkable individuals like William of Glasshampton, George Potter of Peckham and Brother Giles followed. The latter lived among tramps and the homeless in the casual wards of workhouses, making friends 'with men who had no other friend in the world' and enduring every kind of privation with them.

Giles was joined by Douglas Downes, chaplain of Worcester College, Oxford, in founding the Society of St Francis at Flowers Farm, Cerne Abbas, Dorset. Both men inspired the young John as carrying out their vocation in the spirit of St Francis and they became lifelong friends. But he never joined them in their ministry, perhaps because he knew that their way of life could not be combined with his own scholarly work and compulsion to write. Their discipline and devotion appealed to him, but they did not necessitate the ordered and settled ways which were important to him. Later at the Franciscans' house in Cambridge Denis Marsh was to be a particular friend and later still when he became disabled and moved up to Alnmouth John frequently visited him there during his own retirement at Durham.

It was Denis whom he consulted when he was writing *Richest of Poor Men*, published in 1977. Some regard this as one of John's finest books, for its penetrating study of Francis's spirituality reflects his own captivation by the saint. Celano in his *First Life* had called him *ditissimus pauper*, and it was this phrase which caught John's imagination as a succinct summary of the whole character of St Francis. The four foundation-stones of the Franciscan way of life were those listed by Brother Leo in *The Mirror of Perfection*: humility; simplicity; poverty; and prayer. To these must be added obedience – to God and to the teaching of the Gospel – and joy, which was its consequence. Francis himself had given his followers the nickname of *joculatores Domini*, the Lord's minstrels. But, as he insists, 'It would be a mistake to think of St Francis a jolly man, the sort who has a smile for everyone and who regards it as his mission to spread conviviality and happiness.' It was, rather, an inner, spiritual, joy: a deep confidence in the Lord 'that triumphs over weariness and sickness, over the mockery and hostility of others, over misunderstanding and betrayal on the part of friends'. We might add that Alan Paton similarly identified with this from his own experience of South Africa in his meditations on the prayer attributed to St Francis, *Instrument of Thy Peace*.[14]

As regards that prayer, it must have come as a shock to many when John wrote in the *Church Times* of 15 June 1979, that 'no one knows who wrote it'. It does not appear among any of the works of St Francis generally accepted as authentic and was apparently 'first published in a French periodical in January 1913', and circulated among Franciscan tertiaries in Rheims as indicating the sort of person they should be. During World War I it was quickly taken up as a prayer for peace and appeared in the *Osservatore Romano* in 1916. John disliked a later English version in *New Every Morning* (1936) as it replaced the familiar opening of 'Lord, make me an instrument of thy peace', with 'O Eternal God, whose will is our peace'. Although the latter phrase was a quotation from Dante, John felt it important to retain the personal element in this petition: make *me*, let *me*; instead God is being asked to do certain things when in fact we should be asking him to help us to do them. But while the personal emphasis would have appealed to St Francis, the actual sentiments of replacing hatred, discord, doubt and despair with love, unity, truth and hope could, John felt, have been written 'by any Christian who wished to make the world a better place'. So, having denied that there was any-thing specifically Franciscan in the prayer, he goes on to specu-late what kind of prayer Francis might have written. This was not, he recognized, the accepted procedure for an historian, who must be concerned to ascertain facts. However, because the saint was 'unique, an innovator', challenging the standards and values of ordinary secular man, he would have contrasted simplicity with extravagance and luxury, contentment with greed and the desire always to have more, and compassion with indifference to the sufferings of others. John wanted people to think again about the progressive raising of their standard of living, about differentials and comparability, and about the privations of those in the Third World. Not sur-prisingly, then, he was scornful about the facile quotation of the so-called prayer of St Francis by Margaret Thatcher when she won the General Election of 1979.

Shortly before that, his excitement was unbounded when he visited Assisi just days after the bones of St Francis had been exhumed from the stone sarcophagus under the high altar of the Lower Church. 'I saw St Francis!' he exclaimed. After a lifetime's reading and thinking about the saint he could now actually see, and even touch, his bones. There could be little doubt that they were genuine, on both archaeological and medical grounds. Freely admitting that he was not by nature a great lover of relics himself, he added that when he had looked at 'what is commonly passed off as the body of St Clare in the church of Santa Chiara' he had been left cold. The object in Assisi which he had always loved most was the small bit of parchment on which St Francis, with stigmatized hand, had written the blessing of Brother Leo on La Verna. 'I never thought it was possible to get nearer the saint than that. But I must confess that I was deeply moved when I actually saw and handled the very bones of the man who has meant so much to me and to so many others.'[15]

The experience rekindled his efforts to complete his last major work of Franciscana, *Medieval Franciscan Houses*, published in 1983 by St Bonaventure's University, New York, of which he was an honorary Doctor of Letters. Essentially a scholar's reference book, it had originated in terse notes for his own use. Herein he collated, for the first time, into one volume an alphabetical list of some 4500 Franciscan establishments for friars or Clares, from Peking in the East to Cuba in the West, up to the year 1517. Additionally he detailed any significant changes during that period and recorded the names of 'at least some' of those who held office as guardian or abbess. The list was by no means complete, as he admitted, but it was a start.

The work was hailed as 'le travail de géant' by Clément Schmitt OFM in *Archivum Franciscanum Historicum*,[16] while George Marcil OFM commended its usefulness 'through the very magnitude of its concept and its effort at exhaustiveness'. The extraordinary expansion of the Franciscan Order originally noted in the thirteenth century by Celano had likewise been conveyed by John's survey of three centuries. John bequeathed an unpublished card-index which he had assembled over the years of English Franciscan friars to the Franciscan Study Centre in Canterbury, while his complete library of over 2000 books of Franciscana went to St Deiniol's Library, Hawarden. A Moorman scholarship was endowed there to further the work of Franciscan studies in England, to which he himself had so impressively contributed.

## Notes

1. Edited by Cheslyn Jones, Geoffrey Wainwright and Gordon Wakefield (SPCK, 1986).

2. *Theology*, 19.112, (October 1929), pp. 204–9.
3. In ed. Walter Seton, *St Francis of Assisi: 1226–1926: Essays in Commemoration*, (University of London Press, 1926).
4. *Journal of Theological Studies*, 43. 169–70 (January–April 1942), pp. 110–13.
5. October 1941.
6. *Archivum Franciscanum Historicum* 39 (1946).
7. *St Francis of Assisi* (SCM Press, 1950).
8. Letter to John, 4 September 1965.
9. *English Historical Review* 84 (1969), pp. 822–3.
10. *JTS* NS 20 (1969).
11. It has now been further reprinted by Sandpiper Books, Oxford, in 1998.
12. Mowbray, 1974 (new edition, with preface by Cardinal Hume, Mowbrays, 1982).
13. Darton, Longman & Todd, 1977.
14. Fontana Books, 1970.
15. *The Franciscan* (January 1979).
16. *Archivum Franciscanum Historicum* 77 (1984).

# 6

# Bishop in Yorkshire

*Shepherd and Father*

To resign from a benefice or other ecclesiastical appointment could be either courageous or foolhardy, or even both. Whether done for reasons of family, health, scholarship or conscience there is no guarantee of future employment, and few parish priests have sufficient private means to enable them to live without house or stipend. John had already found during the war that it was not easy to get back into the parochial system when he could no longer work on the land. Now, fifteen years later, when he had already been without stipend and cure of souls in Longsleddale for two and a half years, his friends were concerned as to what would become of him. Although both he and Mary could enjoy a modest income from their writings, as well as the additional help of the marriage settlement which G. M. Trevelyan had made upon them in 1930, the situation could not go on indefinitely. Moreover, the Church surely needed to use John's pastoral and administrative gifts in some sphere of leadership. The news in March 1959 that the Queen had offered him the bishopric of Ripon was therefore greeted by many with much joy.

The initial approach from the Prime Minister, Harold Macmillan, on 25 February caused John much heart-searching, as he had grown so used to a 'quiet, scholastic life'. Moreover, he had several uncompleted books on the stocks – his major Franciscan history, as well as a devotional commentary on St Luke's Gospel – and other works planned for the future. So he wrote first to Archbishop Michael Ramsey at

York about 'the battle that has been raging in my mind... You told me that you wanted the next bishop of Ripon to be a scholar, but what does that really mean?' So as to continue to pursue what he believed to be his vocation to write, he asked whether he could be spared committees and the meetings in London which took up so much time. Of course,

> The diocese would always come first, and I should try to do my duty there. I should also hope to play some part in the wider work of the Church. But do you think that I should be justified in making a real stand for the right of a bishop, even in the 20th century, to be also an active scholar?... I very much want to do what is right; but I have always protested against scholars becoming bishops and thus ceasing to be active and productive scholars...

Ramsey replied swiftly and in his own hand: 'What is primarily necessary is a man who has scholarly knowledge of theology and the history of the Church, and will keep his knowledge fresh, and by doing so will (a) be quite naturally a *teacher* as well as a pastor, (b) both in his diocese and in the counsels of the Church help the Church to understand itself and its mission in terms of theology and its own history.' He went on to make the practical suggestion that the period between Christmas and mid-February might be kept free from engagements, excepting only being available for urgent pastoral attention to individuals, so that time could be devoted to uninterrupted study, as he himself had done at Durham and now strove to do in York. Most significant of all, he continued, 'Is our Church to be a *Church*, with a theological and historical understanding of its own nature and mission, or is it to be an institution for the provision of religion? If it is to be the former, the bishops must include men of scholarly knowledge and theological concern: and this freedom needs to be protected. It cannot be done without sacrifices being made, but I dispute the view that all major literary work must necessarily be sacrificed.'

At the same time John travelled down to London to consult

a friend, 'hoping that he would tell me that I might say No'. But in the train he read the Exhortation in the Ordinal, which the bishop addresses to those being ordained to the priesthood, and asked himself whether he could express this ideal more faithfully as a bishop or as a lecturer in Church history. 'When I got to my friend in London I told him that I did not now need his advice. All he said was, "I can see that from the expression on your face." So I accepted, and never for one moment during the last three years have I had the slightest doubt that this is what God wanted me to do.'[1] The Archbishop of Canterbury wrote immediately, 'I am very relieved to know that you have accepted the offer. I can fully understand how torn in heart you were, and, if I may say so, we have really been very anxious to spare you if possible from the distractions of the episcopal office until you had been able to finish your two major works. But we cannot wait as we should often wish to – the pressure was clear that this was an opportunity when the Church ought to turn to you.' He added that both he and the Archbishop of York were anxious not to lay extra burdens upon him. And on the same day, 12 March 1959, the Prime Minister wrote to say that the Queen had been graciously pleased to approve John's nomination, adding 'I am confident that you will justify the choice that Her Majesty has made'. Margaret Deanesley wrote quickly with her congratulations: 'What a lot of sense Mr Macmillan has! We really do need some learned bishops in the Church of England.' And she pondered further, 'Chichester and now Ripon: it does look as if St Wilfrid is taking a benevolent interest in you, doesn't it?' Then Hetty Bell wrote from Canterbury: 'The news did so stir me. George would have been so pleased... I know what a deep and wonderful experience George found in his episcopal work, in particular Ordinations and Confirmations were such truly sacramental experiences with him, and he minded sorely relinquishing them... If you are not already provided for, would you have George's ring? I think he would like you to have it. It is a very plain one, but a nice sapphire stone.' Nothing could have delighted John more, and he was proud to wear it every day for the rest of his life, not least in his own sacramental and ecumenical work.

On all sides the appointment to the See of Ripon was regarded as inspired. It meant that John would be returning to his native Yorkshire, to a diocese covering some 1400 square miles, including the city of Leeds where he was born and many of the dales which were so familiar from his youth and his wartime work. In every way it was a homecoming and John loved being among Yorkshire people again. He chuckled when one of them said, 'You're a dainty man – that's what you are: a very dainty man'. And he himself insisted that he was 'every millimetre a bishop'. His old friend, Lionel du Toit, Dean of Carlisle, preached at his consecration in York Minster on the feast of St Barnabas, 11 June 1959. His sister Theo especially felt then that their mother, who had died three years earlier, was 'present between us. You have inherited from mother that deep and quiet reserve of strength which will be the greatest asset to you in the hard work and trials and problems that lie ahead of you,' she wrote. Then nearly three weeks later, on the feast of St Peter, 29 June, followed John's enthronement in Ripon Cathedral, itself dedicated to St Peter and St Wilfrid, with its fine crypt dating from St Wilfrid's time. Present and past students of Chichester gave John his pastoral staff, made of ebony and silver by Gerald Benney, and inscribed with the words, 'To whom much is given, from him much will be required'. Those words were with him daily for 16 years as he went round the parishes and among the people of the diocese.

John's enthronement sermon in the cathedral where he had received his first commission, as a deacon 30 years previously, had John 21:16 as its text: 'Jesus saith unto him [i.e. Peter], tend my sheep.' It was especially appropriate for one whose work was to 'Be to the flock of Christ a shepherd' in a diocese which had for so long been associated with the nurture of sheep. 'Not only have our dales,' he said, 'given their names to three famous breeds of sheep – Wensleydale, Swaledale, and Teeswater – but the great and noble city of Leeds has for centuries been a centre of the wool trade, even though it now "addles its brass" in many other ways.' The pastoral office of a bishop – caring for the sheep, knowing both them and knowing the Father – could be readily understood then, but he went on to stress its particular importance at this stage of history when attempts were being made to overcome the divisions which had grown up among the flock of Christ. In all this, Anglican insistence on the maintenance of episcopacy was essential, he said, but it meant breaking down the suspicions that it evoked for many.

> We must try to show what episcopacy can be – what, indeed, it was meant to be when, in the springtime of the Church, it grew up as the normal method of administration and pastoral oversight. We must teach people not to *fear* the office of a bishop, but to *love* and *admire* it, and so to *want* it for themselves. Here seems to me a more hopeful approach towards a united Church than all the paper plans and bargains which commissions and conference can offer.

These words were spoken, of course, well before the dramatic development brought about in the ecumenical scene by the involvement of the Roman Catholic Church only a few years later, but they nonetheless put down a marker that ecumenism would be a prime feature of John's episcopate. The other was undoubtedly pastoral, and this, too, was eloquently spelled out in the enthronement sermon. He recalled a conversation he had recently had in the Cumbrian fells with a farmer-shepherd who was working with pick and shovel in the peaty soil, when he had asked, 'Are you doing a bit of draining?' The reply had come, 'Yes, just making it a little better for the sheep'.

> In those words lies my task as your shepherd, 'to make it a little better for the sheep'
>
> - a little easier to believe and trust in the power and immutability of the Eternal God;
>
> - a little easier to carry on when faith is strained and the will grows slack and ineffective;

- a little easier to start again when prayer has been abandoned and the soul has drifted from God;

- a little easier to resist the pressure of society and its mediocre standards of common decency;

- a little easier to keep oneself unspotted from 'the world's slow stain'.

With responsibility for nearly 600 buildings and 250 clergy it would be easy to see the bishop as being 'the managing director of a fairly big concern which owns a lot of property and employs a lot of people', he was once to say to his Diocesan Conference.[2] But this work of administration, even though it entailed meetings of committees which could sometimes be tedious, 'is immensely lightened by the thought that all this has to do with people'. The Church is people, the people of God, and its work is threefold: worship, teaching the faith and mutual fellowship and encouragement in the actual business of living in a world that is indifferent, faithless and even hostile. Thus in his presidential address to his first Diocesan Conference at Harrogate on 20 October 1959 John said,

> We must show men that the work of the Church is not primarily to interest people in religion, nor to provide pious entertainment for those who care for that sort of thing, nor to teach the young to be good citizens, nor to stop people drinking and smoking, nor to balance our parochial and diocesan budgets, nor to do many of the things which absorb so much of our time and energy. The primary duty of the Church is to be the body on earth of the risen and ascended Christ; to make every man, woman and child understand the loathsomeness of sin – in the world, but more particularly in himself; to bring men face to face with both the goodness and the severity of God; to proclaim the Gospel of man's redemption through the shedding of the Saviour's blood; to strengthen weak and sinful men by administering to them the appointed means of grace; to be the agents, ambassadors and stewards of a living, loving,

active and all-powerful God. When we learn to do this we shall not have to worry so much about shortages of men, money or ministry, for we shall be doing the Lord's work, and we know that He will not fail His own.

Significantly, John ended his thirty-eighth and last presidential address on 22 November 1975 with precisely the same words about the primary duty of the Church, for they encapsulated his whole ministry in the diocese. In pursuing it he had been well served by his suffragans, the bishops of Knaresborough. Henry de Candole was already in office when John arrived: he had known him from the Chichester Diocese, where Henry had been vicar of Henfield and Liturgical Missioner. John later wrote of him as 'a son of the Church [whose] interests lay almost wholly in the Church, its worship and its teaching'. A pioneer of the Parish Communion movement, Henry by his teaching and encouragement had helped to transform the life and worship of countless parishes up and down the country. His practice of staying overnight in a parish before the Sunday Eucharist, however, did not appeal to John who preferred to sleep in his own bed and relax in his own home rather than have to fit in with another household. John acknowledged Henry's 'great singleness of heart', and the two men worked well together until Henry retired – though continuing to live in the diocese – in 1965. He was succeeded by Howard Cruse, an Evangelical who had been Vicar of Holy Trinity, Cambridge, and then Provost of Sheffield for 16 years. It was an ideal partnership, coming to a premature end in 1972 because of Howard's recurrent eye troubles. He had been quite content to be a kind of 'episcopal curate', taking on those engagements that John was less anxious to fulfil, and never aspiring to be more than a suffragan. His successor, Ralph Emmerson, who was consecrated on 1 May 1972 in York Minster, was similarly unambitious. Educated at Leeds Grammar School, he had served in several Leeds parishes before becoming Diocesan Missioner and a Residentiary Canon of Ripon Cathedral in 1966. Already known and much loved in the diocese, Ralph came closest to John in a friendship which was maintained until John's death 17 years later.

Other members of John's staff were similarly congenial and loyal: Charles Ellison, and then Alfred Page, as Archdeacons of Leeds; and John Turnbull as Archdeacon of Richmond. Frederick Hughes was Dean of the Cathedral when John arrived; he had been Montgomery's chaplain in the war and is reported to have kept the General up to the mark as a communicant by pointing out that 'Do this in remembrance of Me' was a command, and as such to be obeyed. Hughes was, however, somewhat nonplussed when John sometimes turned up in the Cathedral for sung Evensong on a weekday, as well as coming most mornings a week to the early celebration of Holy Communion. Edwin Le Grice, who came from St Albans Cathedral to succeed Hughes in 1968, was far from feeling threatened by such episcopal devotion and enjoyed a good relationship with John, as well as contributing much to the life of both city and diocese. There were two Registrars (or legal officers) in John's time: Oswy Errington Wilson and John Balmforth; and they accompanied him to all the institutions and inductions of clergy to their parishes. Then there were two highly efficient Diocesan Secretaries in Denis Yates and Peter Driver, although the latter's curtness in correspondence sometimes required a little episcopal or archidiaconal mollification. Driver's admiration for John's presidential addresses to the Diocesan Conference/Synod was such that he had copies sent to every other diocese; and he accepted without question John's overruling, in the interests of the pastoral welfare of a priest and his family, of decisions made by the Pastoral Committee or the Dilapidations Board. He was never a member, however, of the bishop's staff meeting, which was thus entirely clerical; nor did it have regular monthly meetings as would now be the norm. John was always the bishop, and appointments in the diocese, as well as important policy decisions, were made by him. There was no doubt that he was the bishop, and in those pre-synodical days such 'benevolent despotism' [δεσπότης being the familiar word in modern Greek for a bishop] actually worked well, with John's leadership being appreciated by clergy and laity alike.

John felt that his was a happy diocese, with a real family atmosphere in which clergy stayed in their parishes and were not wanting constantly to be on the move. Doubtless some were inevitably overlooked and would have welcomed at least the opportunity to consider a change, while appointments to honorary canonries sometimes caused a raised eyebrow, but this is no different to other dioceses. It is difficult for a bishop to be entirely without a few 'favourites', and John knew this, to the extent of deliberately holding back in showing such preferences. After his first ten years at Ripon he calculated that nearly one-third of the incumbents were in their present livings when he came; indeed one of then, Harry Griffith at Harewood, was ensconced there even before John was ordained 40 years earlier! Moreover, of the 106 men whom he had already ordained to the priesthood, nearly half of them were still in the diocese, or having gone away for a second curacy, had come back again. All this stability created a kind of fellowship of which he felt proud. It was nurtured by the annual Corporate Communion for the Clergy, held in the Cathedral on the Tuesday in Passion Week. These began in 1962, long before the present practice of holding the Chrism Mass and renewal of priestly vows had become widespread. They had an excellent attendance from all over the diocese. John would celebrate and give an address which encouraged the clergy to go forward into the most solemn week of the Church's year when they would lead their people through the saving events which constitute the heart of the Christian faith. Breakfast would follow at the Victoria café, where John and Mary would go round all the tables to have a word with as many of the clergy as possible.

Most of the clergy were instituted to their benefices by John rather than by his suffragan, and this was always the case with newcomers to the diocese. His sermons related to the pastoral work of a priest, deftly portrayed in both the local context and that of the ecclesiastical year. Thus at St John's,

Knaresborough on 30 March 1966, the Wednesday in Passion Week, the priest's ministry was seen in the light of the events of Holy Week. 'Anyone instituted and inducted in Passion Week will begin his ministry at the most dramatic moment in the Church's year. His first job will be to lead his people through the great events of the passion, death and resurrection of Christ. He and they will be very close to Jesus, living with Him through those shattering events which changed the whole course of human history...' He spoke of the three stages of this journey: acclamation, rejection and vindication. All of these would be replicated in the life of the parish priest – he is welcomed with joy, but all too quickly criticized and then rejected as human nature reveals its worst; the priest loses heart, feeling lonely and abandoned, even crucified:

> Sometimes they strew his way
> And his sweet praises sing...
> Then 'Crucify'
> Is all their breath...

That then is the time above all to be 'looking unto Jesus, the author and finisher of our faith, Who for the joy that was set before Him, endured the Cross, despising the shame, and is set down at the right hand of the throne of God'. Priest and people must go on praying for one another as they had done that evening, not losing their vision and sense of purpose as they 'run with patience the race that is set before [them], looking unto Jesus'.

Confirmations and Ordinations were likewise for John, as Hetty Bell said they had been for George, 'truly sacramental experiences'. The former were shared equally with the Bishop of Knaresborough, duly recognizing the claims of both urban and rural parishes. John's addresses were short, simple and direct, usually delivered without notes so that he could look straight at the candidates seated in the front rows. He did not like the girls and women to wear veils, nor was he in favour of boys wearing their uniform: rather all should be cleanly, rather than specially, dressed. He wanted to make the point that

Confirmation was not an event unrelated to ordinary, every-day life, but must become very much part of it.

Ordinands in the diocese speak of letters they received from John during their time of training, as well as of the care that was taken over finding the right 'title' parish for them. Ordinations normally took place in the Cathedral on Trinity Sunday and at Michaelmas, but while John appointed a special preacher for these he invariably conducted the retreat before-hand himself. The necessary legal business and rehearsal were therefore conducted in Ripon on the Thursday afternoon, after which John went down with the candidates to Barrowby, the diocesan retreat house in lower Wharfedale, and stayed with them until the Sunday morning. A junior incumbent would be invited to act as chaplain and look after the arrangements for the services in chapel; one of them records that this experience revived his own ministry at a difficult time. John's addresses were again short and direct, conveying simple truths about God and the work of ministry. On the anniversary of their ordination priests would receive an encouraging letter from their Father-in-God.

John regarded it as of first importance that the clergy should have direct access to him. It was not until his last year, there-fore, and then for special reasons, that he had a domestic chaplain. This meant that in telephoning his bishop a clergyman could get straight through to him if he was at home. If, for instance, he was dictating letters to his secretary at the time, John would usually answer the telephone himself. Clergy also knew that if they wrote to him about a particular problem they could expect a reply by return of post, unless the bishop was away at the time. Even when he was away in Rome for the sessions of the Second Vatican Council his correspond-ence was efficiently maintained because he never lost sight of its pastoral importance. He reckoned that on an average day he would do about 25 letters, mostly dictated by him after breakfast and usually personally signed when he came in from afternoon engagements at about 5 o'clock. Some notes, how-ever, would be written in his own hand. Usually these were about more personal matters for the clergy and their families – the birth or the loss of a child, for example, or a gift of money to help at Christmas or to make a holiday possible. These are still treasured by their recipients to this day. Unseen acts of generosity characterized John's whole life, and as he and Mary had no children themselves they particularly enjoyed treating a clergy family to the Leeds pantomime at Christmas. It took John back to his own childhood, as well as symbolizing the fun there should be within the larger family of the Church. But most of all John and Mary enjoyed entertaining their friends and neighbours at simple evening parties in their own home, Bishop Mount, a fine Victorian house about one mile north of Ripon on the Thirsk road. John, dressed in his black velvet jacket, would show off his rock garden with great pride while guests were having drinks on the terrace, and later there would sometimes be music, with Mary singing and John playing duets – on one memorable occasion with Lady Stevens, the wife of the Vice-Chancellor of Leeds University.

## Leader and Governor

When a bishop is consecrated through the laying-on of hands by the Archbishop and other bishops present, he receives the Holy Spirit 'for the office and work of a bishop in the Church of God'. His ministry, therefore, will be in a sphere wider than the diocese where his chief work of being Father-in-God and shepherd of the flock is to be done. *All* his work, however, must be done 'to the glory of [God's] name, and the edifying and well-governing of [his] Church'. So we look now at John's work as leader in the Church within the diocese and beyond it.

The centrality of worship, its necessary issue in mission and the healing of the tragic divisions within the Church which so hindered its prime work of preaching the Gospel – all these were his paramount concerns. Thus the high-priestly prayer of Jesus as recorded in John 17, 'that they all may be made perfect in one', was very much on his lips and in his heart. As he wrote, 'Christ prays that we may be perfected, "made perfect into one". It is because we are such poor Christians that the Church is divided; and in the long run it is only by becoming better Christians that any real progress will be made towards our goal.'

John's ecumenical work in the wider context of the Church of God will be considered later, but it was complemented by his concern to promote better relations with other Christian denominations within the diocese. When Bishop Dwyer's successor as Roman Catholic Bishop of Leeds was to be appointed in 1966, John wrote to the Apostolic Delegate expressing the hope that it might be someone who would work in the spirit of Vatican II. Thus he was delighted when Gordon Wheeler was appointed. He found him a congenial colleague, sharing a platform with him at meetings during the Week of Prayer for Christian Unity. He allowed Roman Catholic priests to preach in Anglican churches and was himself invited to preach in St Anne's Cathedral, Leeds. Then the possibility of cooperation between the Anglican, Roman Catholic and Free Church chaplaincies to the University of Leeds was discussed at a meeting in September 1970 hosted by Bishop Wheeler at his house in Thorner. Could the different churches work from one site next to Emmanuel Church? An amicable meeting failed to produce during his time the result for which he might have wished, even though it was followed by a five-course lunch cooked by the nuns who kept house for the bishop. 'How very simple they must think our establishment!' he commented in typically Franciscan vein. Three years later, however, he was delighted that the two church secondary schools in Harrogate, St Aidan's and St John Fisher's, established a joint sixth form (September 1973).

John also got on well with Walker Lee, the Methodist Chairman of District for Leeds, talking with him, for instance, about how there could be practical local co-operation between Anglicans and Methodists if the Scheme should fail in the early 1970s (see pp. 123–30). On the down side, however, he was perturbed to hear from a young Methodist probationer who, though not yet ordained, was required to conduct services of

Holy Communion in the seven chapels he was looking after in the dales. 'I did not realise that this sort of thing happened except in an emergency. It does not augur well for union.'

Even more alarming, though, was what the press called 'the Ripon Affair' in early 1967. John had been invited by the Irish Church Association to speak in Belfast about Christian Unity and also to preach in St Anne's Cathedral. But the Revd Ian Paisley and other 'extreme Protestants, almost all non-Anglicans, used this as an opportunity for attacking everything that did not fit in with their ideas'. Worse than that, John was called 'the Pope's quisling', and when interviewed on Ulster television Paisley had said, 'All who saw the Bishop of Ripon could not fail to see the satanic composure on that face'. Despite the promise of police protection, the Dean of St Anne's withdrew the invitation to preach, and in the end John decided not to fulfil the other engagements. Instead he went to Dublin a couple of months later as the guest of George Simms, the Church of Ireland Archbishop, and there he spoke to clergy and theological students on 'The New Ecumenism'. He wrote in his diary, 'I was relieved to find how sensible and tolerant most of the clergy are.' After his return Mary was presented with the honorary degree of Doctor of Letters at Leeds University. In his oration, Professor W. D. B. Grant said, 'Mary Moorman's first book was on William of Orange. We were reading only a month or two ago that the bishop had incurred such odium in certain quarters from attending the Ecumenical Council at Rome as Anglican Observer, that he had had to cancel his visit to Northern Ireland. The shades of Mary's Protestant hero must have fallen enigmatically across the family breakfast table!'

Around the same time John was involved in the Inter-communion Commission, where he pleaded for more theological discussion of the matter and warned against 'taking refuge in practical plans'. In this he was up against the powerful advocacy of Bishop Oliver Tomkins of Bristol, who was chairman of the Commission, and Canon Fenton Morley, the Vicar of Leeds, while enjoying the scholarly support of Canon

Cheslyn Jones, his successor at Chichester. When the report 'Intercommunion Today', appeared in 1968, John felt that it was more concerned with hospitality at Anglican altars than with the real issues involved in Anglicans receiving Communion in other churches. His paramount concern was that 'anticipatory acts of intercommunion on specific occasions', as were being pressed by many, 'would be understood by many more as a gesture affirming the sufficiency of ecclesiastical structures separated from the episcopate'. The very real division between members of the Commission was reflected in the report and its recommendations. The basic questions of what the Eucharist is and who may conduct it still needed to be agreed upon, but John's thinking was thus being prepared for the Anglican–Roman Catholic International Commission (ARCIC) discussions in the following year, and also for the English Anglican–Roman Catholic (ARC) meeting in London in March 1979 when he read a paper on Intercommunion. By then he could build on the Agreed Statements of ARCIC and so suggested that there were four fields to explore: faith, the community of believers; baptism, the community of the baptized; fellowship, κοινωνία, of which the Eucharist is the central point; and sensitivity. With regard to the second, he quoted Professor Adrian Hastings: 'Reasons there must be, and grave ones, in order to withdraw the right of those who share a common baptism from sharing a common Eucharist.' And as to the third field, he took on board the Roman Catholic view that 'eucharistic communion and ecclesial communion are the proper expression of each other and must be kept so'. But he was deeply disturbed by 'a rigid legal system bound by canonical law and strict mandates and prohibitions' which seem 'out of keeping with Christianity and the Gospels'. Pleading thus for sensitivity and charity, he acknowledged that he himself could not really be part of a Church that was so much governed by Canon Law.

John's overriding sensitivity as a pastor was to be shown in the diocese in his advice to the clergy about the admission to Holy Communion of those who had been divorced. In the first instance the Church cannot approve of divorce so long as it upholds the indissolubility of marriage, yet it has pastoral responsibility towards those who fall short of the ideal. In fact, these could well be the people who were most in need of such sacramental grace. Holy Communion was meant to be 'not just a reward for good living, but a means of grace and strength to the weak and sinful'. The three necessary conditions were those laid down in the Prayer Book: 'Ye that do truly and earnestly repent you of your sins' – each party in a divorce must share some of the guilt; 'and are in love and charity' – there must be no bitterness, however bad the other party's behaviour; 'and intend to lead a new life, following the commandments of God' – there must be a positive looking to the future.

On the matter of marriages in church when one of the parties is divorced, John necessarily had to be firm because of the Convocation regulations of 1937, which were still in force even though the law of the land allowed for remarriage, and some clergy took advantage of that. Second marriages, even though they were often the first for a young bride, could not take place in church because of the indissolubility of the marriage bond. A person who had promised before God to observe a life-long union 'till death us do part' could not make the same undertaking a second time. On the other hand, after a civil ceremony has been performed in a Register Office, a couple might have a blessing in church provided that it could not be mistaken for an actual wedding. All this, of course, was before General Synod had authorized a Form of Blessing to be used in such circumstances; and John really would have preferred a simple form of blessing to be conducted in the home of the couple in what would be very much a domestic and family affair. Then, as regards admission to Holy Communion the conditions previously laid down – repentance, charity and the intention to lead a new life – likewise applied.

In 1961 the first part of a fresh translation of the Scriptures, known as *The New English Bible*, was published. It had been 'undertaken with the object of providing English readers, whether familiar with the Bible or not, with a faithful rendering of the best available Greek text into the current speech of our time, and a rendering which should harvest the gains of recent biblical scholarship'. It did not pretend to have the majesty of the Authorized Version of 1611 which lent itself to public reading, but aimed rather to do away with its archaisms. When, however, it was proposed in the York Convocation that permission should be given for the use of the NEB for the reading of the Epistles and Gospels at the Holy Communion, John expressed to his clergy his concern that 'in introducing a new version we are not in fact introducing a new theology'. Others, like T. S. Eliot, had been critical of its somewhat flat style, but John was concerned with significant changes of emphasis which diminished the force of the original. Taking as his example the Epistle for Lent III from Ephesians 5:1-14, the imperative 'Be ye followers of God' becomes 'Try to be like him' – a suggestion or a hope rather than a command. Then 'the wrath of God' becomes 'God's dreadful judgement': 'God's dreadful judgement is what He will do; God's wrath is what He feels. The Christian's attitude towards sin is not primarily a matter of what will happen as a result of it, but of his having grieved God and aroused his wrath.' Furthermore, 'Walk as children of light' becomes 'Live like men who are at home in daylight', obscuring the meaning – 'did it mean night workers, or those who leave work early enough to get home before dark?' – as well as weakening the imperative. Rather than giving a blanket permission for the NEB to be used in place of the AV in the Prayer Book readings, he thus advised the clergy to think carefully about the relative merits of modern translation for each passage. He was equally concerned about the public reading of the Old Testament in the Jerusalem Bible (1966) with its translation of 'Yahweh' for 'the Lord' or 'God'.

In 1964 John entered the House of Lords, having waited his turn for the average five years since his consecration. While undertaking his regular duty of reading prayers, he found that his heavy involvement with the Second Vatican Council until the end of 1965, and thereafter with ARCIC, as well as the considerable distance from Yorkshire which involved staying in London for the week, all made it difficult for him to be more than an occasional attender at other times. But the issues of Homosexual Law Reform and the Abolition of Capital Punishment in the second half of the 1960s naturally led him to support Archbishop Michael Ramsey in his strenuous efforts which won the day for the more liberal and humanitarian view. John's own maiden speech, however, was not until 17 December 1968 when he spoke about road safety. This, he said, was a personal and a moral problem: 'a problem of selfishness, lack of consideration for other people and recklessness. These characteristics of human nature could not be easily cured' – certainly not by fear, by alarmist propaganda, not even by legislation and only partially by education. Poignantly he added, 'We whose job it is to improve human nature know how difficult, and at times heart-breaking, this can be'. More practically, he told their lordships that when tiredness impaired their reactions while driving it was a good thing to take off one's shoes and drive in stockinged feet.

Necessary visits to London were always accompanied by visits to the British Museum or some other library to pursue research connected with his writings, and to facilitate this he would often stay in a small hotel in Bloomsbury, convenient also, of course, for King's Cross, the station to which the trains from York came. He did his duty by attending the regular Bishops' meetings at Lambeth Palace, as well as the meetings of the Church Assembly, later the General Synod, in Church House, Westminster. As regards the former he felt that many of his colleagues were far too concerned to tell the others about what they did in their dioceses, while as regards the latter he felt that there was too much talk and not always well informed. He had a certain impatience with democratic processes in Church government and felt strongly that the Kingdom of God was not going to be advanced by committees and conferences.

He enjoyed, however, the experience of attending the tenth

Lambeth Conference in the summer of 1968. Lasting a month and involving 461 bishops from all over the world, it imbued a great sense of loyalty and pride in the Anglican Communion. 'There was everywhere,' he said, 'a feeling of belonging to something big, imaginative and progressive.' At the same time, though, he asked whether this was consistent with all the schemes of union which were being given an approving nod, and which, if they succeeded, would swallow up large portions of that Communion into a new Church or Churches in which Anglicanism would lose its special characteristics and identity.

John himself was Chairman of sub-committee 29 of the Conference, which considered relations with the Roman Catholic Church. Thus the Conference 'received with gratitude' the Report of the Joint Preparatory Commission (see pp. 113–17), urged the 'speedy continuance' of the Joint Commission on the Theology of Marriage and its Application to Mixed Marriages, and recommended the setting up of a Permanent Joint Commission on Anglican–Roman Catholic relations. Its Resolution 61 gratifyingly expressed 'its willingness to support the Anglican Centre in Rome' (see pp. 108–113), which John had been instrumental in establishing. At the same time, however, in Resolutions 34–35 the Conference affirmed 'its opinion that the theological arguments as at present presented for and against the ordination of women to the priesthood are inconclusive', requesting provinces of the Anglican Communion to 'give careful study' to the issue. John, while feeling that there were 'no fundamental objections' to be made, nevertheless was alarmed at the serious implications which would result if the Anglican Communion, and the Church of England in particular, went ahead in the matter without waiting for the consensus of the Church Universal. He told his Diocesan Synod in February 1974 that the issue was likely not only to be divisive within parishes but was also in danger of setting back the progress which had already been made on the ecumenical front with the two largest Christian Churches – of Rome, and to a lesser extent, of Constantinople. Thus in March 1975 he said to his Synod, 'the day for unilateral decisions on important matters has passed. We are all so much bound up with one another that we ought – wherever possible – to act together and not create new barriers.' He did not go along with the view that it could never be possible to ordain women to the priesthood, but there were practical issues to be thought through. Parishes, for instance, should think realistically about the matter and be asked whether they would be prepared to have a woman as their next vicar. But the ecumenical dimension weighed most heavily with him so that he felt that the time was not right. He was, therefore, not an impossibilist but an inexpedientist.

Diocesan bishops inevitably are drawn outside their dioceses many times a year for meetings in London, but in addition each is usually given a particular external job. Despite his heavy ecumenical responsibilities, John was also asked to become chairman of the Advisory Council for Religious Communities in 1971, and he served in this capacity until 1981, that is, until well after his retirement. Although his particular knowledge and experience was of Franciscanism, as historian and as a medievalist he had a deep appreciation of the religious life, so this new responsibility was far from being a chore. Moreover, he was already Visitor to the Community of All Hallows at Ditchingham, Norfolk, who lived under the Benedictine Rule. Here his wisdom and pastoral sensitivity were much appreciated, as they were also in the matter of the selection of candidates for the priesthood from within a particular religious community. As these were to minister within their community was it necessary for them to undergo the usual ACCM selection conference procedure? Although they were not being ordained for the parochial ministry there was always the possibility they might at a later stage leave their community and expect to be given a parochial post. Fr Alan Harrison, the then secretary of the Advisory Council, records that 'Bishop John guided the long discussion very sensitively to the conclusion that Religious should go through the same process as everyone else, but that in their case there should always be a Religious from another Community as a member of the selection board, to counteract any tendency to be unsympathetic to the Religious Life'. John's homily in the course of a Conference of Religious held in York in 1974 captured the ethos and significance of the Religious Life in his exposition of Romans 5:19: 'As by one man's disobedience many were made sinners, so by the obedience of one shall many be made righteous.' He observed that obedience was the most difficult of the three basic vows, seeing it as far from negative, a saying 'No' to oneself. 'On the contrary, it is a joyful offering, an act of will, an expression of humility. It is not limited to certain known commands, but is the adoption, even though it may be at great cost, of a way of life which we believe to be in accordance with the will of God.' So, just as in Christ the 'obedience of one' wrought man's salvation, so now that work of Christ will be continued by the obedience of many in the religious life.

Very much extra-diocesan, of course, were the overseas visits that John made while he was Bishop of Ripon and which gave another dimension to his time there. The first was made to Malawi in April 1969 at the invitation of Edward Maycock, who had been John's last Vice-Principal at Chichester. The poverty and the friendliness of the people made a deep impression upon him, and he told his Diocesan Conference, 'After reading Missionary Society literature for 50 years or so it is a great thing to see it all for oneself. I wish we could *all* go.' There had been 1500 people in church on Easter Sunday showering him with gifts of cake, rice, eggs, 15 live chickens and a live sheep. On his return to Ripon he raised money to equip the mission hospital at Likoma. A visit to Kenya staying with Archbishop and Mrs Beecher at the end of 1971 was over the Christmas period and was meant to be 'a delayed summer holiday'. It brought home to John the importance of Africanization in the Church so that it could live without a lot of outside help, as well as the need to maintain both evangelistic and ecumenical zeal in a situation where there were so many sects and other religions.

In between the African visits he had been to Luxembourg

and to the United States of America. The latter was in October 1971 to deliver lectures on *The New Ecumenism* at Detroit and Saginaw, to give lectures on Franciscan topics at the Holy Name College, Washington, and to visit Kansas City, Montana and Kalamazoo. In Washington he was able to see Coleman Jennings, who had given such support to Brother Douglas in his Franciscan venture, whilst in Kansas City he saw Bishop Charles Helmsing who had been his co-chairman on the Joint Preparatory Commission (see pp. 113–7). But in the course of travelling 1400 miles in 16 days he observed great contrasts of wealth and poverty in American society and the social effects of drugs, unemployment, bad housing, race and violence which led him to report to his Diocesan Synod that 'The people of the USA are living on a volcano which may blow up at any moment'. But alongside all this there was an optimism and a warm hospitality not least in the churches, which however were characterized by affluence and efficiency as well as a somewhat naïve religious enthusiasm.

Quite different was his trip to Luxembourg in May 1970 for the Fourth International Newman Congress, at which he gave an address at the ecumenical service, referring to Newman as, for Anglicans, 'our greatest disappointment'. Newman had sadly been 'unable to find peace and satisfaction in the Church in which he had been nurtured and to which he was able to give so much'. In his *Apologia* Newman had written, 'I desired a union with Rome, under conditions, Church with Church.' That had not been possible in the nineteenth century, but now ARCIC was beginning to clear the ground for it. After this he went on to Echternacht for the annual commemoration of St Willibrord, the protégé of St Wilfrid, who had taken the Christian faith from Ripon to the Low Countries in the late seventh century. He revelled in walking in the 'Dancing Procession' with Cardinal Alfrink and Archbishop Cardinale, the Apostolic Delegate, and later invited Alfrink to come to Ripon and preach in his cathedral. 'Thank you, good people of Ripon, for sending us the Gospel,' Alfrink was to say so charmingly on that occasion.

In all this full and varied work John never lost the urge to write, as indeed he had foreseen when agonizing about taking up appointment as bishop. Ramsey had reassured him on that score, and although John found that it was not very easy to mark out whole weeks in his diary for scholarly research and writing, he did keep the other end of his desk for his work as 'Doctor Moorman' rather than 'Bishop Moorman'. Mainly at this time he was completing – which also involved considerably shortening – his *magnum opus*, on the Franciscan Order (see pp. 52–4), eventually published in 1968. Before that, however, *The Path to Glory* was published in 1960. This was a commentary on St Luke's Gospel, the fruit of meditations in his days at Chichester and Longsleddale. Like William Temple's *Readings in St John's Gospel*, it combined scholarly with devotional treatment, so that in the words of Michael Ramsey, who reviewed it for the *York Quarterly*,[3] 'The reader is helped to find himself in the presence of the Christ whom St Luke describes, and to feel both the sense of history and the contemporary voice of that history to our present need'. He continued, however, 'As compared with Temple's *St John*, Moorman's *St Luke* contains less elaboration of the expositor's favourite ideas.' We might add, that only a pianist who had actually played in Beethoven's G major concerto could have likened the soft pleading of the persistent widow in Luke 18:1–8 and the 'loud, noisy and emphatic' obduracy of the judge, saying 'No, no, no!', with the slow movement of that work where the soloist gently overcomes the judge's opposition.[4] Another typically Moorman touch is in the story of Martha and Mary in Luke 10:38–42. While the former was up and doing, Mary sat at the Lord's feet: 'This little incident has special significance in these modern days of rush and energy and tension, when there is so little time to listen or to think, with bishops hurrying from conference to conference and clergy running about with their bulging briefcases stuffed with agenda. "Set up a commission," "call a meeting," "arrange a conference," so the cry goes up, so loud, so insistent, that it is hard to hear the voice of the Master: "Sit down... Be still...

Listen."'⁵ Small wonder that one of John's neighbours – the Earl of Swinton, to whom he had given a copy of the book – wrote, 'Thank you so much. I bagged it first. I have been charmed and helped. You do make a chap understand. Thank God and the Prime Minister for sending you here. Don't get translated too soon.' But John was too happy in Yorkshire to take much notice of the speculation in 1966 that he might be translated to Durham when Maurice Harland retired. In true primitive tradition he felt 'married' to his diocese from which he would not have wanted to move.

## Last Year in Office

1975 would have been in any event a significant year for both John and Mary, for in the course of it each would complete their seventieth year – Mary first, in February, and John on 4 June. As things turned out it was to be John's last year in office, an extremely full one and emotionally demanding. It also gives a good picture of what the day-to-day life of a diocesan bishop can be like.

New Year's Day saw John and Mary at their Lakeland home, Hazel Seat, near Ulverston, at the end of their Christmas break. It was wet and misty, making visibility too poor for John to go down to the lake bird-watching, so he stayed in and read some of David Newsome's 'excellent book', *Godliness and Good Learning*. That remarkable phrase from the collect of thanksgiving for William of Wykeham, founder of Winchester College in the fourteenth century, appropriately describes his own character and concerns in and through the oversight of an English diocese, to which he returned that afternoon. After 'a wet drive to Ripon' they found 'a cold and empty house', where the central heating had failed and there had been some damage from recent gales. In the garden, however, some of last year's flowers, roses in particular, were still blooming and spring flowers were coming on apace. More seriously, there were pastoral problems to deal with – the recurring depression of a long-standing friend and a clergy marriage under stress; and a cheque from a lady in Texas for $7500 'for the poor, blind and crippled people of Leeds', provided that none of them was black. He wrote asking for that clause to be withdrawn, and this was eventually agreed. There were letters to dictate next morning before going down to Leeds to discuss what were to be the two major concerns of the year: clergy stipends and pastoral reorganization. They were, of course, linked: the reduction in the number of stipendiary clergy, through retirement and fewer men coming forward to replace them; and the spiralling effects of inflation. Impatient with the Micawber-like attitude of the Stipends Committee that 'something would turn up', John wondered, 'how are the clergy going to feed their children by this time next year?' Encouraged by his Senior Staff, he embarked on a major plan of deploying the clergy over the diocese as a whole giving due weight to the legitimate claims of urban Leeds, with its heavy concentration of population, and those of the rural dales with their more scattered parishes.

Enlisting the help of Thorley Roe, whom he had appointed the previous year to be secretary for Mission and Unity in the diocese and whom he now made also his domestic chaplain (the first in 16 years), he concentrated all his efforts on drawing up his plan so that he could present it to his Rural Deans and the Bishop's Council. The former group he found it natural and easy to work with, whereas the latter he found irksome: 'Forced upon me by the Synodical Government measure, I have to treat them as an important body when I really wish that they didn't exist at all.' He was very positive about the Plan being 'a forward-looking document designed to use more efficiently the resources which we have'. It was an indication that 'the Church is very much alive', and that in Archbishop Coggan's inspired phrase, it was 'stripping itself for action'. Even before publication of the Plan, however, the Vicar and PCC of St Luke's Harrogate had asked to have their large Victorian church declared redundant so that they could worship in the excellent church hall built in the time – and to some extent by the hands – of the previous incumbent.

Cascades of letters came, 'almost all from people who didn't actually go there, but all equally indignant at the idea of its being closed and possibly demolished'. John knew, however, that if church buildings might have to be made redundant in downtown Leeds or up in the dales, then the same must happen in affluent Harrogate.

In February the General Synod meeting in London debated the issue of the Appointment of Clergy and John spoke out strongly against private patronage, preferring the bishop to have as much of it as possible in his own hands or with diocesan boards of patronage. This would enable better deployment of clergy in a time of shortage. However, his amendment that private patronage be abolished was lost, significantly by the narrowest of margins in the House of Bishops. Afterwards he took Eric Kemp, newly appointed to the See of Chichester, to lunch to talk about Anglican–Roman Catholic affairs in the hope that he would take over in due course his work for the Anglican Centre in Rome. But he was becoming more and more reluctant to leave Ripon for meetings in London, arriving late for a bishops' meeting because he was not prepared to travel overnight. Even so, that meant getting up at 6 am, leaving for the train at York at 7 am, in order to be in London by mid-morning. For the same reason he did not go to Canterbury for Donald Coggan's enthronement as this would have meant two nights away from home. He did, however, find Coggan a very much better chairman than Michael Ramsey had been. Undoubtedly John was beginning to feel his age, tiring on those long days which had usually begun at 7.30 am in his cathedral and gave no opportunity for a post-lunch break. In a normal week there would be four or five addresses or sermons to deliver, with an equal number of meetings of diocesan bodies; moreover, there was less and less time for the work of writing which was so essential to his well-being. He did, however, manage to examine for an Edinburgh PhD thesis, and he worked a little on *Franciscan Houses*: 'all these Czech and Hungarian names get one away from the care of all the Churches!' These cares included a difficult problem about exorcism, the case of a curate's wife who had cut the throat of a new-born child, and the question of whether he could license Fr Hugh Bishop, who had been Superior of the Community of the Resurrection at Mirfield and was now living in Leeds with his male friend. John thought that he was now too much of a humanist for him to do so.

Rather more congenial, however, was the University service in Leeds, about which he wrote: 'There is something very pleasant and unsophisticated about these University functions. Everyone seems to want to enjoy the occasion and they are always very friendly towards me, partly because my connection with the University goes back such a long way.' He valued having been a member of the Court and Council of the University and had been gratified to receive the honorary degree of Doctor of Letters, as Mary had been, too. Between them they held five doctorates, as John liked to boast. Later in the year, on 12 November, the Faculty of English dined Mary as one of their Honorary Lecturers, and John, who remarked, 'I was more or less born in the English department and have known seven Vice-Chancellors'.

Mary had her seventieth birthday on 19 February and John gave her some Coalport china, 'the prettiest I could find in London'. He recorded that 'She is wonderfully well and has changed little in the last ten years'. But increasingly his thoughts turned to retirement: Where? And when? The possibility of a house in Durham was attractive, but how could he finance it while still leasing Hazel Seat? A guest night dinner at Trevelyan College in May made the prospect of retirement there more attractive. Realizing that 'it is better to go when they want you to stay than to stay when they want you to go', John nevertheless knew how much he would miss his work with the clergy and the parishes. Yet, 'As I look ahead and around at the many problems which will one day have to be solved it is odd to think that it will be the next Bishop of Ripon who will have to tackle them. This I find hard to believe.' The decision to go at the end of the year, however, was made shortly before his own seventieth birthday in June. A suitable house in Springwell Road, on the edge of Durham, was on the market; moreover, Graythwaite Estates indicated that they did not intend to renew the lease of Hazel Seat at the end of October. Contracts were thus exchanged for the Durham house and possession taken in mid-July. Still without a gardener at Bishop Mount, John had tried to spend as many afternoons a week as he could in keeping that garden under control: now, he reflected, he had three gardens on his hands.

The diocese, however, knew nothing of all this, and John's normal round continued. A typical week was that beginning 11 May: two Confirmations, one in Leeds and the other in the dales, on the Sunday; conducting a 'Quiet Morning' at Barrowby for the clergy of the Harrogate deanery on Monday; giving talks to the Christian Education Movement in Leeds on Tuesday, and to the Methodists in Leyburn on Wednesday; on Thursday lunching with his Examining Chaplains and Post-Ordination Tutors, followed by their annual planning meeting, after which he met with the diocesan education team before going on to a Confirmation at Bishop Monkton, which was followed by a late dinner at the home of one of the adult candidates (whose wife 'must be one of the best cooks in Yorkshire'); and a further Confirmation in Leeds on the Friday evening. During that week also he was, in his spare moments, preparing the lecture he was due to give a week or so later for the Friends of Lambeth Palace Library on G. G. Coulton, the medievalist who had fuelled his interest in St Francis nearly 50 years earlier.

June was a month of anniversaries: his seventieth birthday on the fourth, the sixteenth anniversary of his consecration on the eleventh; and the forty-fifth anniversary of his ordination to the priesthood on the fifteenth. On the first of these he tried to fulfil a longstanding ambition to climb Scafell Pike. Snow high up, however, made progress difficult, added to which his climbing companion lost his shoe. Happily, a second attempt in August was successful: on the way up, he fell into conversation with a young man from Belfast and asked him whether he was Catholic or Protestant? 'He said he was Church of

Ireland, which pleased me.' On the second of these June anniversaries he wrote to Michael Ramsey to thank him for the opportunities he had given him at the Vatican Council, followed by his visit to the Pope and for the work on ARCIC. He told him, too, how much he enjoyed being a bishop. Then the third anniversary was marked by a big celebration in Leeds Parish Church, with a Mozart Mass, some 40 clergy as well as the Lord Mayor. It was immediately followed by the Triennial Festival at Chichester Theological College where he was given a room in the new building, 'a bit like a prison cell'; then up to London for the House of Bishops meeting at which the closure of the College was staved off. At the General Synod on 2 July he was asked to give the blessing at the close of the session as the senior bishop present. The rest, he said, had gone off to the Lord Mayor's banquet at the Mansion House: 'a thing which I have steadily refused to do for the last sixteen years'. Returning to Chichester on 5 July to preach at the nine-hundredth anniversary of the founding of the Cathedral, he enjoyed staying with his friends Jean Bickersteth (widow of Geoffrey, formerly Professor of Italian at Aberdeen), and their daughter Ursula; but found 'talking to endless people' and 'filling in time until the next meal' very tiring. 'Is this a sign of old age?' he asked. Returning to Yorkshire, he was very excited to see the Lady's Slipper Orchid at Kilnsey: 'I stood and gazed at the rarest flower in England', for which he had sought all his life.

Another refreshingly different entry in his diary is for the last day of July: 'While I was getting up this morning I watched a stoat on the lawn dancing, writhing, turning somersaults, leaping about the place, watched by a number of birds who looked perplexed and slightly supercilious. None was foolish enough to get caught, but the stoat put up a magnificent display.' That same day his resignation as from 30 November was announced, one line being given to it in the *Ripon Gazette*, and likewise five days later in *The Times*. Although this was the holiday season, he felt that such brevity was a bit of a snub, or that 'someone had slipped up'. He was amused that a local reporter asked, 'Is your wife going with you to Durham?' But a bad patch of depression followed as he pondered at this slacker time of the year what the implications of it all were.

At the end of August the Anglican–Roman Catholic International Commission met in Oxford to grapple with problems of Authority in the Church. The discussion on Infallibility he felt to be unsatisfactory, with too much 'shadow-boxing'. 'Sooner or later we shall have to speak out or we shall get nowhere.' But the fellowship in the group was good as they had now worked together for six years and formed good friendships. Now they were tackling real difficulties, but John felt that such firm foundations had been laid on the authority of the Church and of ecumenical Councils that the problem was looking far less formidable and forbidding. Professor Henry Chadwick had been particularly helpful and John found it 'a great pleasure to work with him'. For his part, though, Chadwick, who was moving from an Evangelical background to a more Catholic position, was apparently surprised to see what a 'Protestant' stance John sometimes took. By the end of the week John felt that 'we have, to some extent, turned the flank'.

Driving back to Ripon 'at some speed' – 193 miles in as many minutes – he prepared for his last Ordination retreat at Barrowby, complaining of the nylon sheets there and no bed-side light. Then up to Hazel Seat to take down pictures, clean out grates and wash walls and move household things up to Durham. In the midst of it all he came down to Wetherby to take the funeral of its vicar, Wilfrid Marshall, a Leeds boy who had been one of his students at Chichester. He broke the tension by recounting how when Wilfrid was fleeing the College on learning of his failure to pass his exams, the 'minor miracle' of there being no taxis at Chichester station meant that the Principal was having to walk back to the College and so encountered Wilfrid in South Street. Asking him to carry his case for him, he persuaded him not only to spend another night in College, but eventually to re-sit his exams and get ordained. A harvest festival at Romaldkirk followed, with 'a

John Moorman in his study at Springwell Road, Durham with
the Bibliotheca Franciscana in the background, c.1980

John as an undergraduate at Cambridge playing the virginals, c.1927

The Principal going out to bat in the annual cricket match against Salisbury Theological College at Chichester, 1950

John and Mary at Longsleddale before moving to Ripon in June
1959

The Bishop with schoolchildren in Leeds, c.1970

Private audience with Pope Paul VI, Rome 1968

mumbo-jumbo' of harvest hymns: could people not see that
'All is safely gathered in' contradicts the subsequent line, 'the
valleys stand so thick with corn'? Then on to Durham to dig
in the garden of the Moormans' new home: 'There were some
lovely fat worms in the bed which I was digging, and it
occurred to me that these worms really belong to me. I have
never owned any land (or any worms) in my life until I bought
this house. It is a pleasant thought.' Then he and Mary went
bird-watching at Alnmouth, where John had called in to see
Denis Marsh at the Friary: they observed whimbrels, turn-
stones, blacktailer godwits and a Canada goose.

On Michaelmas Day, 29 September, which was incidentally
the Moormans' forty-fifth wedding anniversary, Peter Byrne
and Ros Manktelow from Radio Leeds came to interview John
for a programme about his life and work, particularly his
Franciscan studies and his love of music. He played Bach's
minuet and gigue from the First Partita in B flat: for Mozart,
he said, he would have needed more rehearsal. Listening to the
programme when it was broadcast two days later, John wrote,
'The great moments were when I was heard playing Bach. I
never thought I should come over the air playing the piano.'
Ros later told him how attentively the young engineers had
listened to the talk and how astonished they had been to learn
'that it was me playing the piano and not a record'. Around
that time, too, Ron Kent, the chaplain of the Ripon and York
St John's College of Education came to take John's episcopal
frock coat, breeches and gaiters for the College's dressing-up
box. He said that if they didn't find a play with a bishop in it
they would write one, which again helped John to get through
an emotionally difficult time. 'I am finding this double life very
exhausting,' he wrote, 'trying to write a sermon or see what is
the right thing to do about theological colleges [i.e. at the
Bishops' meeting], while at the same time trying to buy a new
bath and a fireplace and to decide how furniture is to fit in. I
shall be thankful when the next six weeks are over.'
Particularly irksome at this juncture at the end of October was
having to spend five days in London 'to do 25 minutes work –

five minutes a day taking prayers in the House of Lords. I have been a member for about eleven years and done my duty regularly, but I find the debates very tedious. There have been a few moments when I have been thrilled – e.g. the debates on Capital Punishment – but long speeches on the purchase of machine tools and oil pipelines are definitely not for me.' He escaped with Mary to the Turner exhibition – 'What a man! And how astonishing to think that after him came people like Millais and Burne-Jones with their coloured photographs.'

Back then to Ripon for his last month as its bishop. During his 16 years he reckoned that he had preached 1732 sermons and taken 217 institutions, while in 1975 itself he preached 101 sermons – only one of which had been outside the diocese – and gave 20 other speeches and addresses. There had been 12 institutions and licensing services in this year, and 35 Confirmations. Now in the final stretch there were to be four farewell services at strategic centres over the diocese as a whole, his final Presidential Address – his thirty-eighth – at the Diocesan Synod in Harrogate on 22 November, and his last 'Clergy Eucharist' in the Cathedral on 26 November. The text for the first group was that inscribed on his pastoral staff, 'To whomsoever much is given, of him shall much be required', while for the clergy he took the words of St Paul from Acts 20:28, 'Take heed to yourselves and all the flock'. The atmosphere was as poignant as originally at the apostle's farewell at Miletus. After coffee at the Old Deanery John stood at the door and shook hands with each one, and while overt expressions of sorrow were carefully controlled there was a palpable feeling of sadness that 'they would see his face no more (Acts 20:37–38)'. As John wrote, 'Retirement comes very hard on people like me', as he could not come back and see people; and he told Ronnie McFadden, 'It's like having your head cut off.'

A beautiful typed letter, covering two pages, came from Rome – 'To my beloved brother in Christ' – and signed in his own hand,[6] 'Paulus PP VI'. 'It was a splendid letter referring to all my work for Anglican–Roman Catholic unity and on Franciscan history, and sending good wishes for my retirement.' Then on 30 November, Advent Sunday, after taking his last services in the diocese at Roundhay and Whitkirk, he wrote, 'And so it all comes to an end. I still find it difficult to believe that tomorrow I shall no longer be Bishop of Ripon.' As the physically exhausting business of the move to Durham began, the Moormans had their last meal in the diocese with the Ramsdens[6] at Old Sleningford Hall – 'a Right Hon. entertaining a Right Rev. in the kitchen'. Then 'all the familiar rhythms of life disappeared' until they had their 'first fire, first meal and first night' in their new home; but 'I feel as if we were living in someone else's house and am surprised to find pictures and pieces of furniture, which I have known for years, all about the place'. The Bishop of Jarrow and the Rural Dean both called – the latter inviting John to celebrate on Christmas Day at St Oswald's. Cheslyn Jones, on his way further north, called in and gossiped about Chichester for a couple of hours: John found this particularly enjoyable 'now that I have no responsibility for what goes on'. He resumed work on *Franciscan Houses* in his new study, which 'I think I am going to like very much'. On the penultimate day of the year, he wrote, 'In all the turbulence through which we have passed, Edmund Gosse's sad but beautiful book, *Father and Son*, has somehow managed to float to the surface and I spent some time re-reading it.' Sadness and beauty exactly capture the mood of a searing year.

## Notes

1. *Prism* 64 (August 1962).
2. 5 June 1969.
3. November 1960.
4. *The Path to Glory*, p. 209.
5. *The Path to Glory*, p. 128.
6. The Rt Hon. James Ramsden was MP for Harrogate, 1954–74, and Secretary of State for War, 1963–64.

7

## Ecumenical Work

### The Second Vatican Council

The foursquare nature of John's ministry was completed, indeed crowned, by his ecumenical work, first at the Second Vatican Council from 1962 to 1965, and then as a member of the Anglican–Roman Catholic International Commission from 1969 to 1981. As an historian he could have an overview of the sweep of nearly 2000 years of the Church's history, excited by its advance yet pained by its divisions. As an Anglican with a deep concern for truth he had a sense of the delicate balance of scripture, reason and tradition which was needed to achieve it. As a former Theological College Principal and now as a diocesan bishop he was concerned to build up the Church in faith and pastoral care. It was as if in it all he had made his own the charge given to St Francis in the little church of San Damiano, 'Rebuild my Church'.

Unlike San Damiano in the early thirteenth century, the Church of God in the mid-twentieth century was not collapsing in ruin, but there could be no doubt that its witness was severely hampered by its 'unhappy divisions'. The oldest and most serious of these was that between the Eastern Church centred on Constantinople and that of the West based on Rome. Largely this had come about because of the fundamentally different ways of thinking between Greek and Latin, reinforced by the political situation of the first millennium, so that 1054, the official date of the beginning of the Schism, completed, rather than originated, the break. Councils held at Lyons in 1274 and Florence in 1439 failed to effect more than a temporary mending of the breach. Then, in the sixteenth century, came the fragmentation of the Church in the West. New developments like the Renaissance of classical learning and humanism, as well as the growth of national and lay power, were to have an inevitable impact on the hegemony of the medieval papacy. Moreover, the much-needed reform of abuses within the Church was delayed until after the 'protest' of Luther, Zwingli and Calvin had been made and Europe effectively divided between Catholic and Protestant.

Even more tragic was the way in which these European divisions were transported to the rest of the world in the missionary expansion of the nineteenth century to Africa and the Far East. The International Missionary Conference held at Edinburgh in 1910 was called to address this, and can be said to have begun the Ecumenical Movement of the twentieth century. Archbishop William Temple was to call it 'the great new fact of our era'. Gathering momentum through the horror of two world wars, it resulted in the inauguration of the World Council of Churches at Amsterdam in 1948, in which one of John's heroes, George Bell, played a major part. The movement, however, was incomplete without the involvement of the Roman Catholic Church, and it is easily forgotten that as long ago as 1908 the Lambeth Conference of Anglican bishops had made the momentous statement:

> There can be no fulfilment of the Divine Purpose in any scheme of reunion which does not ultimately include the great Latin Church of the West, with which our history has been so closely associated in the past, and to which we are still bound by many ties of common faith and tradition.

Unfortunately, however, the Roman Catholic Church's view was that unity already existed within itself and thus it was simply a matter of all others returning to the true Church and submitting to the authority of Rome. Even the new Pope, John XXIII, who, though aged 77 when elected in 1958, was quickly through his charismatic personality making an impact on the whole world, took the same line as Pius XI and Pius XII had before him by addressing other Christians as 'separated brethren'. 'Let us call you sons and brothers,' he engagingly said. 'Allow us in our fatherly and loving heart to cherish the hope for your return... Observe, we beg of you, that when we lovingly invite you to the unity of the Church, we are inviting you not to the home of a stranger, but to your own, your Father's, house.'[1]

Marvellously, it was the same Pope who, within three months of his election, announced to a startled world that he intended to summon a council – the first since 1870 – which would be concerned with two great issues, *Aggiornamento* and *Ecumenismo* (renewal and reunion). Here, as Moorman was to write, 'was a real turning-point in Church history, a sign of the entry of the Roman Catholic Church into ecumenical discussion, the inauguration of a new era in Church relations'.[2] Moreover, exciting as that was in itself, it was to be even more so for him personally when Archbishop Michael Ramsey responded promptly to the Vatican's invitation to send observers to the Council, due to begin in October 1962, by asking John to be the senior Anglican representative.[3] It was an inspired choice: John's knowledge of Latin and Italian, his historian's perspective and his convinced Anglicanism all combined to qualify him admirably and he threw himself whole-heartedly into the work. It entailed his being in Rome for the greater part of the four sessions of the Council in the autumns of 1962–65. With the strident exception of one incumbent, who was almost paranoid in his public criticism of his bishop, the diocese was proud to think that through their diocesan they were to have a ringside seat, as it were, and John was diligent in keeping his people informed of the Council's progress by means of the monthly diocesan newsletter and his presidential address at the half-yearly Diocesan Conference. He also kept a journal of his time in Rome and lodged this at Lambeth Palace.

Within a short while after the completion of the Council he was to publish *Vatican Observed: An Anglican Impression of Vatican II*.[4] Here, in about 200 pages, he gives an immensely readable account of the debates of the Council and an assessment of its Constitutions and Decrees, seasoned with humorous asides and perceptive comments about some of the participants. Most of these were doubtless familiar with written Latin, but to hear it spoken with so many different accents was confusing without the benefit of simultaneous translation. Cardinal Cushing of Boston, however, had never learnt any Latin, and John was amused to hear him say, 'I can't understand a word these guys say. I just have to look intelligent and get someone afterwards to tell me what it's all about.' At the same time he was full of admiration for Maximos IV, the Melkite patriarch, who wished to speak in Aramaic, the language of Our Lord himself, but after a while resorted to French. At the age of 86 he was nevertheless in John's view far more up to date on pressing issues, such as family planning, than the majority. But his greatest admiration was for Archbishop Montini of Milan, one of the first Cardinals to be created by Pope John but, before the Second Session of the Council, elected to succeed him in St Peter's chair. Whereas John felt that John XXIII had stumbled on the idea of the Council through 'a kind of divine intuition', without realizing what its implications might be, Paul VI on the other hand was only too aware of its potential both as regards achievement as well as difficulty.

The hospitality given to the Observers and the friendliness shown to them all was most gratifying, all the more so in view of the fact that their presence was itself an innovation. Not only were they given prime seats in the tribune of St Longinus, where they could be easily seen by the Pope who acknowledged them as he entered, but also they were well looked after by Mgr Arrighi of the Secretariat for Unity, who produced summaries of the previous day's proceedings and arranged weekly meetings with some of the *periti*. They were thus able to express their thoughts on major issues, albeit without any opportunity to address the Council themselves. Cardinal (then just Mgr) Willebrands, however, told John at the end of the First Session of the Council, 'The presence of the Observers here is very important. You have no idea how much they are influencing the work of the Council.'[5] John himself quickly became well-known in Rome: in his purple cassock and with his slight stature he was easily distinguishable among the numerous and almost unknown Roman Catholic bishops from all over the world. He enjoyed, too, being addressed as *Eccellenza* in hotels and restaurants. Later on during the Council, when Mary went out to Rome for a while, she quickly overcame her strongly Protestant hackles and delighted in acting as hostess at receptions and small dinner parties which the Moormans gave for some of the Cardinals as well as the other Observers.

John shared in the general optimism which surrounded the Council at its outset, though this did not prevent him from being realistic about 'the tough barrier' that existed between the Churches. He likened this to 'the wall of Berlin, dividing one world from another'.[6] Indeed, Archbishop Ramsey had written to him a couple of months earlier singling out the sensitive issues of mixed marriages, the bitterness which would be caused by the canonizing of the Elizabethan martyrs, and 'the wrongness of the Roman Catholics in re-baptising converts (as they frequently do) since this undermines the "one baptism" which is the sticking-point of unity'. Expectancy, coupled with stout realism, thus characterized John at the beginning of what he regarded as the most momentous event of his life, wherein he was to witness history being made.

The opening service lasted 5½ hours – 'the longest I have ever attended. Yet, though something of an endurance test, it was never boring.' The assembly was vast, with roughly 2300 bishops from every continent. 'Never before had so large and so representative a body of Churchmen been assembled together in one building.' Moreover, 'no one had ever been present at a General Council before'.[7] Much then would depend on the commissions responsible for producing draft texts and for revising them in the light of debate. Preliminary work had necessarily been done by preparatory commissions, but if it had been expected that they would be reappointed then it soon appeared that an articulate 'northern European bloc', led by Cardinals Liénart of Lille and Frings of Cologne, found this unacceptable. Their concern was to make the commissions more representative geographically as well as theologically, and above all, independent of the Holy Office. 'The first shots had been fired,' wrote John. 'The first "no" had been said.' His excitement increased when further 'noes' were registered in debates on the Liturgy and the Sources of Revelation. The traditionalists put up a strong case for leaving things as they had been, with the Latin Mass as laid down at the Council of Trent (1545–64); also with equal value given to Scripture and Tradition, as 'the double source of revelation'. Observers like Professors Oscar Cullmann of Basle and Paris, and F. C. Grant of Union Theological Seminary in New York, were appalled at what they heard, as it took no account of the progress which had been made over the past century in biblical scholarship, in which Roman Catholic scholars too had played a constructive part. After the conservative rulings of the early life of the Biblical Commission which Leo XIII had established in 1902, Pius XII's encyclical *Divino Afflante Spiritu* (1943) had reflected a more positive attitude towards biblical criticism; then in 1954 the secretary of the Biblical Commission conceded 'full freedom' to Roman Catholic scholars in matters of literacy and historical criticism in all areas where faith and morals were not involved.

Cardinal Frings led the attack, finding that 'what is here of inspiration and inerrancy is at once offensive to our separated brethren in Christ and harmful to the proper liberty required in any scientific procedure'. Then it was Bishop de Smedt of Bruges who delivered the *coup de grace* by stressing the disastrous ecumenical implications of the stance, which 'would not encourage dialogue... or represent progress, but a retreat'. Most disastrous of all he said, 'a great, an immense hope' would be destroyed: 'the hope of those who, like Pope John XXIII, are waiting in prayer and fasting for an important and significant step finally to be made in the direction of fraternal unity, the unity of those for whom Christ our Lord offered this prayer: *ut unum sint*'. Not only was this received with immense applause, but Moorman was to regard it as 'perhaps the most important speech of the whole Council'. The Church of Rome had been saved from making itself the laughing-stock of the academic world; and with such evidence of 'liberal and progressive thought in the Church, there is very real hope for the future'.[8] When the decree returned later in revised form during the Third Session of the Council, Cullmann was delighted to hear 'this marvellous phrase' that 'in the Holy Scriptures, the Father who is in heaven constantly meets his children and speaks with them'.[9] Abbot Butler of Downside was to say:

> In the course of this almost miraculous Council we have done much to drive out that spirit of fear and excessive anxiety by which at times our labours were hindered. Today I say: Let us not be afraid of scholarly and historical truth. Let us not be afraid that one truth may tell against another truth. Let us not be afraid that our scholars may be lacking in loyalty to the Church and to traditional doctrine. One of two things is true: *either* there is a world-wide conspiracy of scholars to undermine the bases of the Christian faith (and a man who can believe that can believe anything); *or* the aim of our scholars is to reach the full, objective and real truth of the Gospel tradition.

He insisted that 'What we want is not the childish comfort which comes from averting our gaze from the truth, but a truly critical scholarship which will enable us to enter into "dialogue" with non-Catholic scholars'.[10]

Butler later commented to John that whereas the first session of Vatican II had shown that there was 'a liberal minority' in the bishops, the second session had shown that this liberal minority was much larger than had at first been thought, while the third session had shown in fact that it was a majority. John was fascinated to observe how this groundswell affected the subsequent constitutions. That on the Liturgy was gratifying in the way in which it was catching up with Anglicanism in its concern to use the vernacular, to place greater emphasis on the Bible and preaching, to emphasize the corporate nature of the eucharistic action and to enable congregational participation. In these ways they might even 'triumphantly invent the Book of Common Prayer'!

'Excellent in principle, but rather cautious in practice', was his verdict, and he could not disguise his disappointment that the giving of Communion in both kinds was severely limited to very special occasions to be determined by the Apostolic See.[11] The withholding of the chalice from the laity was one of the great divides in Eucharistic worship between Rome and the rest of the Christian world, and John had strongly hoped that what he saw to be obedience to Our Lord's command, 'Drink ye all of this', would have been observed as in the first 13 centuries of the Church. Nevertheless 'a great advance towards unity' had been made so that 'it is now difficult to distinguish between a R.C. Mass and an Anglican Eucharist'. Moreover, within the decade the Agreed Statement on the Eucharist issued by the Anglican–Roman Catholic International Commission at Windsor in 1971, would show both Churches as believing in the Eucharist as the sacrifice of Christ and of His true presence in the sacrament. 'Agreeing on the nature of the Eucharist, and celebrating almost identical rites, has brought the two Communions much closer together than they have been in the last 450 years since the breach with Rome.' Here was 'a real step forward in the ecumenical sphere'.

On 3 June 1963 Pope John XXIII died, throwing the future of the Council into some uncertainty, as a Council can only be summoned by a Pope. The progressives were sufficiently in the ascendant, however, for the Sacred College to elect Cardinal Montini of Milan as the new Pope. Taking the title of Paul VI he quickly indicated that he wished the Council to continue. 'Only John could have started the Council,' one French bishop said, 'only Paul can finish it.' But would Montini be assertive enough in leadership? Moorman saw Paul VI as a scholar and a statesman, cautious and calculating, but he was thrilled by his speech at the opening service of the Second Session of the

Council on Michaelmas Day, 1963. The nature of the Church and its place in the world of today was singled out as the greatest issue which the Council must face. What, then, is the Church? And what is its mission? Moreover, who can draw its boundaries and say who is in and who is out? The Pope reminded the assembly that this latter question, the problem of ecumenism and the place within the divine economy of those who were now politely termed the 'separated brethren', would have to be faced. 'The Council aims at complete and universal ecumenicity,' he said, 'that is at least what it desires, what it prays and prepares for. Today it does so in the hope that tomorrow it may see the reality.' He thanked the Observers, 'representatives of the Christian denominations separated from the Catholic Church', for their presence and participation. Then came the courageous expression, with voice trembling, of 'the deep sadness we feel at their prolonged separation'. He continued even more poignantly and courageously, 'If we are in any way to blame for that separation, we humbly beg God's forgiveness and ask pardon too of our brethren who feel themselves to have been injured by us. For our part, we willingly forgive the injuries which the Catholic Church has suffered, and forget the grief endured through the long series of dissension and separations.' This was not only a great moment, but, so far as John knew, 'the first occasion on which Rome had offered anything in the nature of an apology to other Christians'. Sadly, when a year later at the British Council of Churches' conference at Nottingham, John was among those who tried to get that assembly to reciprocate such charitable and forgiving words by thanking the Pope and the Council for what they were doing for ecumenism, the suggestion was turned down, apparently with acclamation from some. Then euphorically but quite unrealistically Nottingham proceeded to issue the rallying-call for 'reunion by 1980'. As John saw it, this could at best produce three Churches, not one; a pan-Protestant one, alongside the Roman Catholic and the Orthodox Churches, and the aim of 'presenting an undivided Christ to the world' would still not have been achieved.

'He added "the coming great church" may be "coming" but it doesn't look very "great", since at best it could not contain more than thirty per cent of the Christian population of the world.'[12]

Gratified and humbled as he was by Paul VI's epoch-making words, John was nevertheless sorry to hear the Pope speaking of 'the unique fold' of Christ's Church into which 'the many sheep of Christ who are not at present within' are being called. It was repeating John XXIII's aspiration that non-Catholics would return to the 'one fold and one shepherd', based on the unfortunate translation of John 10:16 in both the Vulgate and the Authorized Version of 1611. John pointed out that the original Greek uses the word ποίμνη, meaning 'flock', in the second part of the verse, so that it reads in modern translations – such as the Revised Standard Version and the Jerusalem Bible – 'so there shall be one flock and one shepherd'. The former farm-labourer saw how crucial this more accurate reading was for ecumenism, for as he pointed out,

> A fold is an enclosure, built of stone, wood, or corrugated iron; while a flock is a group of living creatures, in this case, sheep... So long as people think of the Church as fold, with walls which can be high and doors which can be shut, then there is not much to be done except to urge those outside to come in. But if we begin to adopt the idea of a flock, not all members of which are of one fold, then we enter into the realm of relationship, of communion, which may at present be partial, imperfect or incomplete, but which can grow if we have the will to nourish it.[13]

He was to rejoice, therefore, that the Constitution on the Church (often known as *Lumen Gentium* from its opening words), declared, 'God has gathered together as one *all* [his italics] those who in faith look upon Jesus as the author of salvation and the source of unity and peace, and established *them* as the Church', reversing statements made by previous Popes and identifying with the Book of Common Prayer's assertion that the Church is 'the blessed company of all faithful people'. A unity already exists among all who have been baptized, 'for all bear what a Yorkshire shepherd would call his "spot"'. Paragraph 3 of the *Decree on Ecumenism* read, 'Men who believe in Christ and have been properly baptized are brought into a certain, though imperfect communion with the Catholic Church', for while there are differences in some matters of belief, there exists 'a hierarchy of truths' which differentiates between the common faith of all who call themselves Christians and the lesser differences which separate them.

There were two areas in which the Council in its discussion of the Church as the People of God might have exacerbated those differences: the place of Mary and the authority of the Pope. As regards the former, John was relieved that instead of declaring, as had been mooted, Mary as 'Co-Redemptorix' and 'Mediatrix of all graces', she was seen within the context of her divine Son and of the Church 'of which she is both type and pre-eminent member', as Abbot Butler said. He was personally happy to accept Pope Paul's designation of Mary as 'Mother of the Church'. After all, the Anglican theologian, Dr R. H. Lightfoot, in his commentary on John's Gospel, had written, 'Mary, the Lord's physical mother now becomes, at the Lord's bidding and as a result of his work, the spiritual mother of all those who are or are to be re-born in him.'[14] To which John adds, 'If the Church is the fellowship of those "reborn in Christ" – as the Evangelicals say – then there is a proper sense in which Mary can be called the Mother of the Church.' John commented, 'Now that the Roman Church has done so much to try to "contain" its Mariology, it is to be hoped that non-Roman Churches may be encouraged to take another look at their teaching on this important subject.' The tendency in the past to be negative about it or to ignore the matter altogether was to be deplored.

The issue of papal infallibility had similar potential for divisiveness among Christians. Its promulgation at the First Vatican Council in 1870 could have made the summoning of any subsequent Council unnecessary, if not impossible. Thus when John was discussing the Council with a group of monks at Ampleforth – only a short distance out of his diocese – and had been asked what surprised him most about the Council, he said, 'That it should have been held at all.' Like most people he had seen Vatican I as 'the Council to end all Councils', for if the Pope is infallible then what need was there for a council? However, it could be argued that the work of Vatican I had been cut short by the invasion of Rome in 1870, leaving undone a consideration of the place of bishops within the Church. Now nearly a century later a Pope was asking the assembled bishops 'to develop the doctrine regarding the episcopate, its function and its relationship with Peter'. Moreover, he let fall the word 'collaboration', which raised hopes that the concept of 'collegiality' might gain general acceptance. John was amused to hear Cardinal Cushing say that if a College of Bishops was what was wanted, he would raise the money for it; but the idea of the Pope working with and through the bishops of the worldwide Church, such as had been posited in the Conciliar Movement of the later Middle Ages, was exciting. 'We in the Observers' box received this with considerable satisfaction since the whole issue had obvious ecumenical implications,' wrote John. 'We welcomed it as a corrective to the doctrine of Papal Infallibility, which can now be seen in proportion. Authority in the future will rest not with the Pope alone but with the episcopate, the apostles, together with their leader.' If authority is thus spread out over the whole episcopate, but with the Pope, guided by the Holy Spirit, making final decisions, then 'the old bugbear of Papal Infallibility looked a little less alarming'.[15]

After the long debate on the Church came quite naturally one on Ecumenism, of particular interest to all the Observers and not least to John. As Professor Howard Root, who had now joined the Observers, has written, 'Historians may one day agree that the debate on the Decree on Ecumenism, during the Second Session of the Council, was in some ways more important than the final text of the decree itself. It raised far more questions than the decree answers, but it opened doors which no decree could close.'[16] Far and away the most significant of these arose from chapter 3, 'Christians separated from the Catholic Church'. Its first section dealt very appreciatively with the worship, spirituality and religious life of the Eastern Churches, but its second section referred to 'Christian Communities arising from the sixteenth century onwards'. John records how, when the Anglican Observers read this they expressed their concern that their Church had been omitted from the *Schema*. 'It was clearly not one of the Oriental Churches, but equally clearly it could not have been said to have "arisen" in the sixteenth Century, since it was the ancient Church of the English people, catholic but reformed.' Recognizing that a very large number of the bishops present were either ignorant of Anglicanism, or perhaps baffled by it, John was gratified when in the course of the debate two French bishops, Collin of Digne, and Gouyon, coadjutor of Rennes, said that they looked in vain 'for any clear allusion to the great Anglican communion, which in its origins is certainly quite distinct and different from the communities of the Reformation'. Even more impressive was Abbot Butler who thought it 'altogether appropriate' that there should be special mention of the Anglican Church which was 'so widespread, so devoted to patristic antiquity, and which has deserved so well of the ecumenical movement'. Bishop Green of Port Elizabeth then went even further and asked for a reconsideration at highest level of the issue of the validity of Anglican Orders. But a sour note was struck by Bishop Dwyer of Leeds – John's opposite number in Yorkshire – who, in the light of the recent publication of *A Quaker View of Sex* and Bishop John Robinson's *Honest to God*, questioned the faith and morals of Christians in England. In spite of this intervention, the Secretariat for Unity revised the *Schema* so that it now spoke of the Churches which had separated from Rome and 'among those in which Catholic traditions and institutions in part survive, the Anglican Communion stands out'. Later, so as not to offend the Old Catholics, the latter phrase was changed to 'the Anglican Communion occupies a special place', and in this form was accepted by the Council.[17] 'A special place' – these were heady words and John could not fail to be excited by them, and even to take some credit for them.[18] But what was their implication for the future?

'By 1964,' John wrote, 'the fun [i.e. of the Council] was beginning to wear off.' There was 'the same grind all over again', 'another three months away from the diocese', and 'no new experiences to look forward to'.[19] The expectancy of the First Session and the thrill of 'having a crack at the Curia', followed by the real breakthrough of the Second Session as regards Collegiality and Ecumenism, was followed by the Third Session in which feelings ran high. He recalled that 'Twice the Council was really angry, more angry than I ever saw it, and both times over a very controversial but essential document – on Religious Liberty', discussion of which had been twice deferred. This had prompted 17 cardinals to appeal directly to the Pope, beginning their letter with the phrase, *magno cum dolore*. Underlying it all was a real struggle between the conservative Curia and the progressives. Xavier Rynne wrote that 'the spirit of joyous expectation' of the Johannine era had now been followed by a time when hopes 'seem to have been dampened by the more timorous and cautious Pauline spirit'.[20] If Pope John had thrown open the windows of the Church to let in fresh air, was Paul now 'checking the thermometer lest any cold drafts seep in'?

John regarded the Declaration on Religious Liberty – *Dignitatis Humanae* – as 'the most controversial document of the whole Council because it raised the question of the development of doctrine, which was strongly opposed'. But he was gratified that the Pope himself saw it as one of the major texts of the Council. In recognizing the dignity of the human person, it acknowledges his right to exercise his religion and to hold fast to the truth as he sees it: no one is to be 'restrained from acting in accordance with his own beliefs'. Parents, for instance, have the right to decide the kind of religious education their children are to be given. But how did this square with the requirements that children born of a mixed marriage should be baptized and educated as Roman Catholics? Instructions issued from the Holy Office on 18 March 1966, that is after the conclusion of the Council, showed that in practice no change was being made, despite Cardinal Heenan's suggestion that, whereas the rules should normally be strict, special regulations might be drawn up to make things easier where one of the partners in a marriage is a practising member of another Christian Church. John strongly felt that if this was not done then 'a serious blow will have been struck to confidence in the Roman Catholic Church's wish to be on better terms with her neighbours or to take seriously her own statements about Religious Liberty'.[21]

Further disappointment was to come when the Pastoral Constitution on the Church in the Modern World – *Gaudium et Spes* – was presented. Early on in the Council, Cardinal Suenens had insisted that the Church must look outwards and help the world in facing the immense problems of peace and war, poverty and hunger, the population explosion, racism, atheistic regimes, and so on. As a result a further two years was spent on drawing up a new *Schema* by a commission under Bishop Guano, with Fr Bernard Häring CSSR, the distinguished moral theologian, as its secretary. A lengthy document of 35,000 words was produced, which John felt was pedestrian and so generalized in its first part as to be almost banal. While it perhaps tried to say too much, its second part did not say enough in order to give that 'clear lead' which was constantly being asked of the Church, particularly on such issues as contraception and nuclear warfare – 'the pill and the bomb'. The Fathers of the Council were as much divided on these as was the world outside; moreover, on the former it was known that the Pope was appointing a special commission to look at the whole problem from theological, moral, medical and psychological standpoints.[22] John reflected that 'it would have been better if those who compiled this *Schema* had asked not so much for the attention of "the separated brethren" as for their collaboration'.[23] As it was, the final text he felt, 'will not solve the world's problems, but it may help to make people think more deeply about them; and if it does that, it will have achieved something.'[24]

In early December 1965 the Council was brought to a conclusion with two big services in St Peter's. Preceding them, however, was one held at the Church of St Paul's-without-the-walls on 4 December, which was entirely the Pope's own idea. The Observers were invited not just to attend but actively to participate through the reading of lessons and the singing of the *Magnificat* and 'Now thank we all our God'. In a moving address Paul VI thanked the Observers in French for their co-operation in the Council, saying how their departure would 'leave a loneliness around us which we knew nothing of before the Council but which now saddens us: we would like to see you with us always!' Afterwards John, on behalf of them all, spoke of the 'deep debt of gratitude' which the Observers owed to both Pope John and now Pope Paul in their being treated as 'honoured guests'. He also paid tribute to the Secretariat for Promoting Christian Unity 'under the leadership of our good friends Cardinal Bea and Bishop Willebrands' for facilitating their understanding of the Council and its work. But whereas 'The Council is drawing to its end... the work for Christian Unity is but beginning', and 'with the entry of the Roman Catholic Church into this field... the Ecumenical Movement has taken on a new dimension. At last we can say that the whole Christian world is engaged in the search for that unity for which Our Blessed Lord prayed.' He pointed to the Decree on Ecumenism, the Constitution on the Church, the Declaration on Religious Liberty and the Decree on the Missionary Activity of the Church as together forming 'a basis on which future dialogue and co-operation can proceed'. For all this 'we are deeply thankful. But,' he continued, 'may I express the hope that, having done so much, the Church of Rome will be willing to go further and do her best to take away, so far as she can, those barriers which still remain between us, and which are such serious obstacles to the attainment of unity.'

The draft of this speech had actually specified those barriers as being 'the laws which govern mixed marriages, the painful custom of giving at least conditional baptism to those who are converted to the Roman Catholic faith, and rivalries in the mission field which can only hinder the progress of the Gospel of Christ. I know that all of us cherish the hope that, in the years to come, the Roman Catholic Church will see her way to removing some of these barriers which, in our minds, do so much to foster that spirit of fear and mistrust which we all hope to dispel.' And if he had been speaking for Anglicans only he would have added that just as the anathemas and excommunications imposed at the time of the breach between East and West in 1054 had now been lifted, perhaps the Bull *Regnans in excelsis* of Pope Pius V in 1570 excommunicating Queen Elizabeth I of England might be 'committed to oblivion'.[25] Even more, that the Bull *Apostolicae Curae*, of Pope Leo XIII in 1896, which declared Anglican orders to be 'absolutely null and void', might be rescinded.

John's sense of history and concern for truth ensured that a strong realism balanced his natural excitement in experiencing the Council and assessing what it had achieved. He would surely have been gratified by the way that his own contribution was acknowledged by Cardinal Willebrands and Père Duprey in their letter to Mary at the time of his death. Writing of the 'very personal contribution' John had made to the cause of Christian unity, they added, 'His work as the principal Anglican Observer at the Second Vatican Council was effective because of the special gifts of scholarship and spirituality on which he was able to draw.'

## The Anglican Centre

The Council had accomplished an immense amount, so that Bernard and Margaret Pawley could write, 'The Anglican Observers... came away from the Council, not to indulge in fanciful dreams about the future, but soberly thankful that so much had been achieved in so short a time against so much opposition'.[26] John himself, however, saw that much still needed to be done and was particularly concerned now that it should in fact be done. As a start he felt that it was essential that Anglicanism, and its worldwide spread in the Anglican Communion, should be better known and understood in Rome, especially as it had been acknowledged as having 'a special place'. Both he and Canon Pawley, who since 1960 had been the Archbishop's first representative in Rome, had received many enquiries about it during the time of the Council. John felt, therefore, that what was now needed was a Centre with an office and a chapel, rooms for meetings, and most significantly of all, a library of Anglican history, theology, spirituality, liturgy and missionary activity. In November 1965 he discussed this possibility with John Findlow, who was to come out to Rome as Pawley's successor, and John Satterthwaite, at that time the Secretary to the Council on Foreign Relations at Lambeth Palace.

Princess Orietta Doria-Pamphilj, whose mother and grandmother were English, and her English husband, Frank Pogson Doria-Pamphilj, had come to know the Pawleys and the Anglican Observers very well during the time of the Council and had been generous in their hospitality. When they heard that an Anglican Centre was being thought about they offered a flat in the Palazzo Doria at a privileged rent of 200,000 lire (then £115) a month, including rates, with heating and lighting additional. The Palazzo stands on the Via del Corso, in the very centre of Rome, so John lost no time in taking Bernard Pawley, who had returned to Rome for the last weeks of the Council, to see it. Then a couple of days later he took Archdeacon Douglas Wanstall, the Chaplain at All Saints' (Anglican) church in Rome, and Miss Virginia Johnstone, who had been Pawley's secretary and was now to work with John Findlow, for a further opinion. All agreed that the opportunity was too good to miss and John quickly got the keen support of Archbishop Ramsey. He then wrote to Bishop Ralph Dean, the Executive Officer of the Anglican Communion, to get wider support for the project. John Findlow, whose base as Secretary to the Commission on Roman Catholic Relations was at Lambeth Palace, was then asked to help set up the Centre and become its first Director.

The apartment in the Palazzo Doria was taken over officially in early 1966. John asked Ramsey if there could be a special vote in the Church Assembly as 'it would give me a chance to speak about it'. The financing of the venture was always to be a problem and, knowing this, Mary was to leave a very substantial sum for the Centre in her will. John regarded as his own personal contribution to the enterprise the collecting of books for the library. An initial £5000 was needed to stock it, and he appealed for this through the Church newspapers. He sought the co-operation of religious publishers and communities, canvassing authors and friends to donate copies of their own books. He himself arranged the first accessions on the shelves, recording in his diary for 2 October 1970, 'we have now about 6000 volumes, almost every one of which has passed through my hands'. Later he enlisted the help of Professor Henry Chadwick in surveying the balance of the library's contents, and Canon John Halliburton in monitoring accessions. He was very gratified when Lady Fisher gave 189 of the late Archbishop's books to the library in 1973, and even more pleased when the total number of books reached over five figures.

In March 1966 Archbishop Ramsey went to Rome to visit the Pope who welcomed him and his entourage, which included Bishop Ralph Dean, 'not as strangers or foreigners but as fellow-citizens with the saints and of the household of God'. At this historic meeting in the Sistine Chapel Paul VI also said, 'You are rebuilding a bridge, which for centuries has lain fallen, between the Church of Rome and the Church of Canterbury: a bridge of respect, of esteem and of charity. You cross over this yet unstable viaduct, still under construction, with spontaneous initiative and safe confidence...' On the previous evening Ramsey dedicated the Anglican Centre in Rome to be 'a place where Christians of different traditions can meet and come to know one another', adding that 'such personal knowledge and understanding plays a vital part in ecumenical work'. He then continued with these important words:

> The Anglican Communion cherishes the Holy Scriptures and the Catholic Creeds. In history, it values the lessons of the Reformation of the sixteenth century, and it values no less the continuity which it claims with the ancient Church. In spirituality, it learns from saints and teachers of its own, while it also tries to learn from saints and teachers of every period in the West and in the East. In theology, it learns from the Scriptures, the ancient fathers and the liturgy, while it strives to use whatever light is shed by modern knowledge upon the understanding of man and the world. The Anglican student is often a debtor to writers within the Roman Catholic Church. This Centre is an attempt to repay the debt by making available the resources of Anglican learning to any who will come and enjoy them.

Next month, in April 1966, the Anglican Communion as a whole, through its Consultative Body meeting in Jerusalem, sponsored the venture, and its Executive Officer, Bishop Ralph Dean, was made chairman of the Centre's Council. John Findlow was succeeded later as Director by Harry Smythe in 1970, who in turn was followed by Professor Howard Root from 1980 to 1991.

The actual opening of the Centre was on 5 October 1966, when Bishop Willebrands in the presence of Cardinal Bea and other dignitaries, both Anglican and Roman Catholic, gave the inaugural lecture in French, stressing the ecumenical significance of Archbishop Ramsey's visit to the Pope earlier in the year. Showing a remarkably accurate understanding of the Anglican Communion, which he spoke of as a 'communion within the one holy, catholic, and apostolic Church', he first of all gave full weight to the historic visit of Archbishop Geoffrey Fisher to Pope John XXIII on 2 December 1960 – the first by an Archbishop of Canterbury since that of Thomas Arundel in 1397; a time when, of course, there was 'full and perfect communion' between Ecclesia Anglicana and Rome. Fisher's

visit was seen by Willebrands as 'a response to the announce-
ment of the creation of the Secretariat for Unity' and resulted
in the appointment of Canon Bernard Pawley as the representative of the two English archbishops to the Pope. Now
Ramsey's visit was to widen this representation by making
Canon John Findlow the representative of the Archbishop of
Canterbury 'as chairman of the Lambeth Conference'. It was
the Anglican Communion as a whole with which dialogue on
the basis of the recently concluded Vatican Council's texts was
to be entered with Rome. 'Theology after the Council of
Trent,' he said, 'was characterised by opposition... The consequence was withdrawal and partiality in the explanation of
one's own doctrine and in judgement of the other. The other
side was the enemy... rather than the brother. Today, thanks
to God, all this has changed... It is above all the brother.' He
went on to echo words of Paul VI that 'knowledge will bring
us to charity, and charity will bring us to unity', as well as the
often expressed insistence of Michael Ramsey that truth must
be the basis for unity, 'unity in the truth'. So now in brotherly
love and concern for the truth this new Anglican Centre would
be a place where common traditions, as well as different
traditions, could be explored.

Willebrands then went on to reflect that the Council's
document on Ecumenism had spoken of *fratres disjuncti*,
avoiding the expression *fratres separati*. 'Disjointed' rather
than 'separated' brothers: for whereas 'separated' meant 'a
rupture which goes to the root, "disjointed" means there is
a failure, a lack of full communion, but there remains communion on the basis of baptism, the faith, prayer and the
Bible'. Thus, Willebrands insisted,

> there is a great deal which remains common to us all. There
> is at the same time a basis and tradition that unites us and
> there are traditions that separate us. The Holy Father said
> that it is a good method to find a starting-point in those
> things which unite us in order to find the possibility of sur-
> mounting everything which separates us... I think that this

Centre, which is the immediate fruit of the visit of His Grace to His Holiness, will contribute by research, by studies, by conversation, to the dialogue which will be developed in the immediate future. It will contribute by personal contact, by thought, by prayer. There is a chapel in this Centre, a library and rooms which will be a means of arriving at that unity – even in plurality and in many forms – at unity in Christ. The basis and the accomplishment must be Christ present amongst us by His Word, by His Sacraments, and above all by the crown and accomplishment of the Sacrament of the Eucharist. He waits there at that table which is not yet common to us. It is offered by Him as a table of fellowship. It is already sought after by us as such.

No words could have better expressed for John his vision for this Centre which he had worked so hard to establish. They reverberate now, over 30 years later, as the Centre is being moved to more spacious and accessible premises within the same Palazzo Doria where, in the words of Canon Bruce Ruddock, its present Director, its ministry 'is increasingly important today rather than the reverse'. Therefore it is to be hoped that the appeal launched by its Trustees to facilitate its move and refurbishment, as well as its endowment for the future, will allow the name and work of Moorman to have a continuing memorial. In that way the 'special place' of Anglicanism may become more than just a pious phrase.

## 'A Serious Dialogue'

The Common Declaration by Pope Paul VI and the Archbishop of Canterbury at St Paul's without-the-walls on 24 March 1966 announced their intention 'to inaugurate between the Roman Catholic Church and the Anglican Communion a serious dialogue which, founded on the Gospels and the ancient common traditions, may lead to that unity in truth, for which Christ prayed'.[27] That dialogue, they said, should include 'not only theological matters such as Scripture,

Tradition and Liturgy, but also matters of practical difficulty felt on either side'. Accordingly, in May 1966 Bishop Willebrands went to Lambeth to discuss the setting up of a Joint Preparatory Commission with Archbishop Ramsey, who then on 30 June wrote to John asking him 'to be the Anglican-Chairman of this body and I greatly hope that you will be able to say "yes"'. John replied, 'I will do what I can. But please see that there are some good theologians to compensate for my lack of theology.' Thus it was announced in November that the other Anglican members of the Commission would be Bishops Glyn Simon of Llandaff, Harold de Soysa of Colombo and Edward Knapp-Fisher of Pretoria; while Professor Howard Root, Canon James Atkinson and Canon Eric Kemp came from the theological faculties of Southampton, Hull and Oxford respectively, along with Professor Eugene Fairweather of Toronto and Dr Massey Shepherd, Jr, from California. Nine Roman Catholics with similar episcopal and/or academic backgrounds were appointed by Rome, with Bishop Helmsing of Kansas City as their chairman. One of these, Fr (now Professor) Adrian Hastings, has since written that 'the English members very largely made the running so that here at last was a top-level episcopal and theological confrontation (amicable yet also often quite sharp) not only between world or continental Catholicism and Anglicanism but also very positively between the Anglicanism of England and the Catholicism of England'.[28]

The Commission's task was 'to prepare the scope and subject matter of theological dialogue between the two Communions', and John in a preliminary meeting with Willebrands in October 1966 had stressed that this must not be 'historical discourse' because 'we do not start from zero'. Now was the time for real dialogue, and at the first meeting of the Commission at Gazzada in northern Italy in January 1967, he and Willebrands started proceedings by reading papers on 'Why is dialogue now possible?' John bluntly said, 'because we have gone on long enough in our separate compartments and because the Roman attitude towards the problem of Christian

Unity has changed so much in the last five years', so that many Anglicans have now become interested in the possibility of union with Rome. Willebrands, for his part, emphasized the biblical, liturgical and social renewal which had taken place in the last 40 years or so in the Roman Catholic Church, thus creating a new context in which to talk. They were followed by Professor Fairweather and Fr Michael Richards (of St Edmund's, Ware) on 'Where should dialogue begin?' 'To an *enlarged* Church,' suggested the latter. Free and frank discussion followed on a variety of theological issues and practical problems, with 'the study of the theology of marriage and its application to mixed marriages' being singled out as requiring the setting-up of a separate joint commission. Above all, members were 'humbly grateful for the sense of urgency and Divine guidance throughout the conference'. One of them specifically commented that 'perhaps the chief memory of the meeting is that here was not a leisurely approach to academic dialogue, but a dynamic meeting of very earnest and determined men bent upon healing wounds that had festered for too long'.[29] And the press-release of 12 January 1967 boldly began with the words, 'After 400 years of separation between the Roman Catholic and Anglican Churches, official representatives from both have taken the first steps towards restoring full unity.' Apparently John himself insisted on that arresting first sentence.[30]

In the same spirit of urgency and friendship two further meetings of the Commission were held within the year: at the end of August at Huntercombe Manor, Bucks, and in Malta at the very end of December. Their outcome was the Malta Report, dated 2 January 1968, in which 'the truly decisive note was set for the new and "special" relationship'.[31] The ultimate objective of organic unity between Canterbury and Rome might be achieved, as Bishop Henry McAdoo suggested, by 'staged engagement or phased rapprochement', and to this end the joint use of buildings, the sharing of facilities for theological education, co-operation in liturgical renewal, as well as joint or parallel statements from Church leaders on 'urgent

human issues' were to be encouraged. Ecumenical co-
operation in missionary activity was recognized to present
greater difficulty, while it was urged that 'the question of
accepting some measure of sacramental intercommunion apart
from full visible unity' should be addressed. That required
'both a true sharing in faith and the mutual recognition of
ministry'. Of course, this raised the issue of Anglican Orders,
but that must be considered in the context of the theology of
the ministry, which in turn had to be considered in the context
of the theology of the Church. Then beyond that, 'A serious
theological examination should be jointly undertaken on the
nature of authority' in such matters as 'the unity and
indefectibility of the Church and its teaching authority, the
Petrine primacy, infallibility, and Mariological definitions'.[32]
Eucharist, Ministry and Authority – these were the three big
issues which a permanent joint commission should, and in the
event did, address, with the results to be seen in the ARCIC
reports of 1971–81.

But first the Malta Report had to be received by the heads of
the two Churches who had set up the Commission. Ramsey,
looking ahead to the Lambeth Conference which was to meet
that summer, had already sent copies in confidence to all the
Anglican metropolitans, asking for their comments. By Easter
these had all been received, with the exception of that from
Japan, but Rome continued to be silent. Canon Purdy has
revealed that 'In the first week of April the SPCU [Secretariat
for Promoting Christian Unity] was informed from the
Secretariat of State that the document had been "lost"', so he
himself took a duplicate copy round by hand to the Vatican,
along with 'anxious letters from England'.[33] John likewise went
out to Rome with two of his clergy, and, accompanied
by Bishop Willebrands, had a special audience with the Pope
on 29 April 1968. The Holy Father was most cordial in his
welcome of an old friend, but seemed tired and preoccupied: as
was learned later, this was the very time when he was
agonizing about *Humanae Vitae*. John commented that he was
'extremely vague about the Report', but later told his Diocesan

Conference that his own intervention was 'perhaps the only occasion when an Anglican bishop has intervened successfully in papal policy'.[34] Purdy, however, has since revealed that further delicate machinations behind the scenes were necessary before the members of the Lambeth Conference were able to receive copies of the Report even 'in pamphlet form', albeit accompanied by a letter from Cardinal Bea and Bishop Willebrands to the Archbishop of Canterbury, dated 10 June 1968. Although official permission had not been given for the general publication of the Report – and in the end never was – the Pope's gratitude was expressed for the work of the Joint Preparatory Commission and his agreement that a Permanent Joint Commission should now be set up to carry out the dialogue between the two Churches along the lines laid down in the Report. Two months later the Lambeth Conference[35] recommended the setting up of such a Commission, representative of the Anglican Communion as a whole, and urged the 'speedy continuance' of the Joint Commission on the Theology of Marriage and its Application to Mixed Marriages.

In many ways the Malta Report can be seen as the high watermark of Anglican–Roman Catholic relations. John proudly quoted to his Diocesan Conference the words of the press-release, that this document 'stands out as containing the first formal joint statement ever made of the faith we rejoice to share'. And he went on to say that to have got thus far 'is a sign of the ecumenical spirit which is blowing now through all the parts and portions of the Christian Church, and which compels us to look again at even the most difficult and obstinate of the problems which keep us apart'.[36] In a similar vein, Professor Hastings observed that the Commission worked speedily, enjoying a great deal of publicity, 'and hence helped to generate a powerful sense of momentum at a time when within the Church as a whole, a positive tide was still flowing strongly'.[37] Why, then, was Rome so wary about its publication? Was it, as he suggests, because the possibility of partial intercommunion had been mooted as a stage towards 'full, organic unity' pending the resolution of theological differences? He then concludes that 'The Malta Report may be fairly seen as the last, and perhaps most generous expression of the mood of optimism prevailing in the Catholic [*sic*] Church in the years immediately following the Council'. That mood had, in his view, by the end of 1968 'been transformed into one of dominant confrontation and pessimism'. Nevertheless, the Report's 'cautiously radical proposals... did in fact light the way, not only for the slow grind of theological discussion carried on by ARCIC, but also for the vast popular Anglican/Catholic realignment which was now going on at ground level across the world'. Rather differently, Canon Purdy comments, 'the great majority of both Anglicans and Roman Catholics were going to find that "common inheritance" and "living tradition", and the prospect of "extensive sharing", were ambitious ideas which went against the feelings in their bones'.[38] And he suggests that 'Nowhere was this more evident than in the British Isles', and records that even Michael Ramsey thought that the wording of the Malta Report asking for 'an official and explicit affirmation of mutual recognition from the highest authorities of each communion' as they acknowledged their shared faith was premature and even naïve.[39]

It was against this background that each Church now embarked on the process of selecting suitable members of what would be known as the Anglican–Roman Catholic International Commission, balancing the requirements of geographical spread, theological expertise and pastoral experience, as well as ensuring a certain degree of continuity with the Joint Preparatory Commission. John was invited to serve not only for the latter reason, but also because of his invaluable experience of the Second Vatican Council; he was, however, not to be co-chairman. Henry McAdoo, then Bishop of Ossory and later Archbishop of Dublin, had an unrivalled knowledge of classic Anglicanism as formulated by the Caroline divines of the seventeenth century, which Ramsey felt qualified him to be the Anglican co-chairman. Additional theological weight was supplied to the Anglican team by Professor Henry Chadwick, who had been Regius Professor of Divinity at Oxford and was now the holder of the parallel chair at Cambridge. John was more than happy to continue as a member of the team rather than as its leader with the additional work and possible stress that this might involve. The annual meetings of the Commission for ten days at the end of August and into September each year fitted well into his diocesan programme and indeed gave him a wider vision for his own more local ministry in Yorkshire. It also gave him a broader canvas when issues like Synodical Government and the Anglican–Methodist Scheme were being discussed. 'We Anglicans – especially in England – suffer from living in too small a world,' he told his Diocesan Conference in November 1966.

John's presidential addresses to the Ripon Diocesan Synod faithfully informed his people of what was happening in ARCIC, but also recorded his own excitement at being involved in what he felt to be an epoch-making exercise. Throughout it all he never lost that vision of the two great Communions recovering their former unity, in obedience to the divine imperatives 'that they may all be one' and 'that the world may believe'. Thus on 19 October 1974 he told the members of his Diocesan Synod:

It is because I believe that such a thing as Christian Unity *is* possible – however formidable the obstacles – that I am prepared to work with the International Commission in trying to discover what each Church *really* believes and whether the divide is quite so great as we sometimes think... I am certain that there is hope of progress. A new generation of Roman Catholic theologians is growing up, far more liberal and co-operative than anything we have known in the past. It is because of this that I believe that our work is infinitely worthwhile. I do not expect quick results. I doubt if I shall live to see the coming together of our two great Churches. But if I can make some small contribution towards the healing of the wound which has kept us apart for 400 years, then I shall say my *Nunc Dimittis* with joy.

The Commission's work was undoubtedly helped by being residential, with the fellowship experienced at meal-times and the opportunity of informal discussion. More than that, the Commission's programme provided for joint daily worship. Anglican and Roman Catholic Eucharists alternated, with each side attending each others' services but only making their Communion when one of their own number was the celebrant.

The first-fruits of the Commission's work came in the 'breakthrough' of positive agreement between the two Churches on Eucharistic doctrine as expressed in the Windsor Statement of 1971. Issues like the eucharistic sacrifice and the real presence of Christ which had been so divisive in the sixteenth century – indeed, for which men and women had given their lives – were seen to be no longer so. John told his Diocesan Synod in February 1972 that it was 'the most important statement made since the Reformation', at the same time quoting the opposed views of both the Catholic Priests' Association and the Protestant Truth Society. The former saw it as 'a painful and ignominious exhibition of lack of courage and lack of faith', while the latter saw it as 'a clear reversal of Reformation principles, and a departure from those great scriptural truths for which the Reformation martyrs died'. When Mr Kensit asked John to oppose it in the General Synod, 'I told him he had written to the wrong man'. Not only did the Statement express all that he had always believed about the Eucharist, but also he was gratified by the affirmation which it received in the Roman Catholic periodical *The Month* (February 1972). 'The members of the Commission', it said, 'are men of eminence and unimpeachable authority. They are well known for their commitment to the ecumenical cause, but by no stretch of the imagination could they be described as wild-eyed and woolly-headed enthusiasts.' Nevertheless, John recognized that it would take a long time before ordinary people in the pews of their local churches would absorb it.

The Commission, however, pressed on with its work and in September 1973 at Canterbury was able to produce an Agreed Statement on Ministry and Ordination. By returning to the

New Testament the Commission was able to agree 'that ministerial *office* [my italics] played an essential part in the life of the Church in its first century and we believe that ministry of this kind is part of God's design for his people'. Furthermore, it was able to agree that 'Just as the formation of the canon of the New Testament was a process incomplete until the second half of the second century, so also the full emergence of the three-fold ministry of bishop, presbyter and deacon required a longer period than the apostolic age. Thereafter this threefold structure became universal in the Church.' Thus, and not least in its use of the word 'presbyter' rather than 'priest', the Commission was able to cut through the controversies of the Reformation era and to offer 'a positive contribution to the reconciliation of our Churches and their ministries'.

There were, however, many issues concerned with 'authority, its nature, exercise and implications' which still needed to be thrashed out, and these, along with *Elucidations* of the previous Agreed Statements, took the Commission up to 1981. John, however, retired as Bishop of Ripon at the end of November 1975, and so might have thought that he would be replaced on the Commission soon after. Archbishop Coggan, however, wrote in September, 'I know that it would give great satisfaction to the members of ARCIC, and not least to their Chairmen, if you felt able to continue. I suppose that the main burden of their work will be over within the next two years.' Thus John was involved in the work of ARCIC I (as it came to be called, in distinction from the new Commission which later succeeded it) for a further six years – in fact, until its Final Report was produced at Windsor in 1981.

The crucial issue in this period was that of Authority in the Church: as the first Statement on the subject issued at Venice in 1976 observed, 'It was precisely in the problem of papal primacy that our historical divisions found their unhappy origin'.[40] Recognizing that the 'consensus' already reached in fact represented 'the ideal of the Church as willed by Christ' and the way in which history showed a failure to achieve it, it acknowledged that 'common recognition of Roman primacy' would bring changes to *both* Churches. 'Communion with the See of Rome would bring to the churches of the Anglican Communion not only a wider *koinonia* but also a strengthening of the power to realise its traditional ideal of diversity in unity. Roman Catholics, on their side, would be enriched by the presence of a particular tradition of spirituality and scholarship, the lack of which has deprived the Roman Catholic Church of a precious element in the Christian heritage.'[41] Further to that amazing comment, it was stated that the Roman Church could learn much from the 'Anglican synodical tradition of involving the laity in the life and mission of the Church'. While, therefore, 'the basic principles of primacy' had been agreed, there still remained the particular problems of the Petrine texts, the 'divine right' of the papacy, the infallibility of the Pope and his universal immediate jurisdiction, which would be the subjects of dialogue culminating in the Authority II statement at Windsor. There the need of 'a universal primacy in a united Church' was agreed, also that conciliarity was complementary to it as a 'multiple, dispersed authority'. But as standpoints in both Churches were not 'destined to remain static' it was asserted that 'some difficulties will not be wholly resolved until a practical initiative has been taken and our two Churches have lived together more visibly in the one *koinonia*'.[42]

As Professor Adrian Hastings has written, 'A very carefully laid theological basis now existed for a considerable advance towards full communion between the two Churches, at least to some degree of the "intercommunion" which had been explicitly put forward as an intermediate goal by the Malta Report in 1968'.[43] The Final Report of ARCIC I in its Conclusion reckoned that the convergence reflected therein 'would appear to call for the establishing of a new relationship between our Churches as a next stage in the journey towards Christian unity'.[44] Precisely what that 'new relationship' would entail was not clear to all then, nor is it now, but it certainly represented John's deep awareness of the divine imperatives for unity, which still continue to urge us on.

## Schemes of Reunion

If John could be seen as 'a principal bridge-builder between Rome and Canterbury',[45] there were some who saw him as a wrecker in other ecumenical spheres. He was, for instance, sceptical about the Faith and Order Conference of the British Council of Churches held in Nottingham in 1964 with its shibboleth of 'reunion by 1980'. Professor Hastings has called it 'the most important specifically English ecumenical conference ever to be held'[46] – significantly not at Oxbridge but in a modern secular university – at which, moreover, Roman Catholic observers were present: 'a very great step forward in English terms'.[47] John, however, felt that its large membership of 500 people representative of all the non-Roman Catholic denominations in England was too unwieldy for the sharp theological dialogue to which he had become accustomed on ARCIC. More than that, it was not competent for such serious discussion since those with theological expertise were heavily outnumbered by youthful enthusiasts whose sense of urgency was such that they demanded action rather than talk. Most alarming of all, however, in the envisioned 'One Church Renewed for Mission' was his realization that 'at the very least there would be two Churches – the United Church which the British Council of Churches hopes to bring about, and the Roman Catholic. So that any talk about *one* Church, or about "presenting an undivided Christ to the world" is still premature.' So he encouraged his Diocesan Conference in November 1964 to look 'Romewards' where what he called 'the other Ecumenical Movement' was taking place.

It was against the same backdrop that he also viewed the proposals being made in the Anglican–Methodist Scheme of 1968. Conversations between the two Churches had been going on since the early 1950s, leading to an Interim Statement (1958) and a fuller Report five years later. A two-stage programme for the reunion of Anglicans and Methodists was proposed: the final goal of 'union in one Church' being firmly seen as the second stage, to be preceded by 'a stage lasting for some years at which our two Churches enter upon full communion with one another, while retaining their distinct life and identity'. This first stage was necessitated by various administrative and legal factors, not least Establishment. In 1965 the Convocations of the Church of England and the Methodist Conference 'gave conditional acceptance, as a basis for further negotiation' to the 1963 proposals and set up the Anglican-Methodist Unity Commission to make plans for their implementation. In particular the Commission was asked to revise the Service of Reconciliation of the respective ministries and to prepare an Ordinal to be used in both Churches from the beginning of Stage One. John thus told his Diocesan Conference in May 1965 that although the 'general wish of the Church as a whole' was to bring about such a union, 'it would be idle to suppose that "organic union", even with the Methodists, is something which it will be easy to bring about'. He had deliberately said 'even with the Methodists' because in so many ways Anglicans were nearer to them than any other body, not least because less than 200 years divided them. What had begun as a reform movement within the Church of England, with John Wesley himself urging his followers to 'be Church of England men still. Do not cast away the peculiar glory which God hath put upon you', this had gradually drifted apart from the parent body, and in the subsequent period both had changed considerably. Although episcopacy might at first sight seem to be the problem, John felt that eucharistic doctrine and the ministry were more difficult issues. The real heart of the matter lay in differing conceptions of priesthood, involving the 'power and authority to perform certain acts which lay people are not empowered to do. These acts are concerned with the Eucharist and Absolution.' While the Church of England had been very careful to retain the threefold ministry of bishops, priests and deacons empowered and authorized through the historic episcopate, Methodism's emphasis was on the 'priesthood of all believers' which authorized such particular ministry as was locally required, without any sense of continuity or permanence. The crux of the whole matter, therefore, was whether any 'Service of Reconciliation' could overcome these differences without completely fudging the issue. He did not disguise his doubts about this and firmly said at the outset that he would prefer to see mutual ordination as the way forward.

With the publication of the proposed *Ordinal* and *The Scheme* for Anglican-Methodist Unity in 1968 the time for final decision had come. The Lambeth Conference that summer welcomed the proposals, and wanted to express its belief that 'the Service of Reconciliation is theologically adequate to achieve its declared intentions of reconciling the two Churches and integrating their ministries'. However, some bishops from Australia and elsewhere had been unable to get hold of copies at home and had since had no time to examine them closely as to their theological principles. A more general resolution, which all could accept without detailed study of the Report, was then presented by the Bishop of Jarrow and accepted. The Metropolitan of India, the Most Reverend Lukasa de Mel, however, violently castigated this timorousness and was loudly clapped, though John commented that 'a good many bishops realized, on closer reflection, that he had been grossly unfair in what he had said'. So strongly did he feel about this intervention that he absented himself from the final service of the Conference in St Paul's Cathedral at which Metropolitan de Mel was to preach. He wrote to tell Archbishop Ramsey of his intention, even though he realized that his absence would probably not have been noticed or questioned. Ramsey, however, replied in his own hand:

My dear John,
    One expects to carry away from a Lambeth Conference things to regret and things to be very thankful for – but this time I find myself with a *wound*, given to me by your note saying that you would not come to the closing Eucharist with us because (so I gathered) you disapproved of the preacher. I regretted that speech by the Metropolitan of India and thought it hurtful and unfair.

But I thought that in the same discussion *you* touched a
feebly low level when you told the Conference that you
knew a better way of promoting Anglican-Methodist
union – as if you really know one, why have you withheld
it from us your English colleagues who are struggling with
the problem? 'Collegiality'! However these disagreements
are a continuous part of our existence and it is only that
breach of fellowship which wounds.

Yours ever,

Michael Cantuar.

John yielded to none in his admiration – and indeed affection
– for Ramsey, and was distressed to learn how much he had
hurt him. 'The last thing in the world that I would wish to do
would be to give you pain', he replied, 'and if I have done so I
am very sorry. I think that last week many of us were, perhaps
inevitably, on edge – tired and to some extent depressed – by
the way in which things were going. In the midst of it all came
the very unfortunate, and as you say unfair, speech by de Mel
in which he caused much distress to some of my best friends,
including George Simms whom he most unjustly attacked for
something which was not his responsibility...' He went on to
say that he might again have been upset by de Mel's sermon
'in which case I could not have joined in the service as I should
wish to do', and that 'the only *honest* thing to do was to say
why I felt it better to stop away, though with great reluctance'.
He then went on to refer to his own contribution to the debate:

I felt that the 'alternatives' set out in the Report are
knocked down in a rather cavalier manner, and that some
plan along the lines of CSI [Church of South India, 1947]
ought to be considered before a final decision is made. I
was going to say this in my speech (which was carefully
timed to be within the limit of 7 minutes), but the bell
rang and I had to leave much out. When the Scheme is
debated in Convocation I shall have to say what I think,
but so far have had no opportunity of discussing it... I

fear that the Church is going to have a very difficult time during the next year or so. Division there is bound to be, and I pray every day for wisdom and charity. Again may I say how truly sorry I am if I have grieved you. We have been such good friends in the past that we must not allow a difference of opinion to injure our fellowship and affection.

With love,

John.

However, John was not alone in finding the proposed Ordinal satisfactory but the Service of Reconciliation ambiguous. The Bishop of Peterborough, Cyril Eastaugh, wrote to say that although he did not wish to prejudice the minds of his clergy, 'I am with you in finding it less and less possible to take part in the Service of Reconciliation... I get constant requests for a lead in this matter. In the interests of truth it will have to be given before long... We most certainly ought to debate this without tension, to be given time to do it and propose an alternative scheme. After all, we are being asked to make an irreversible decision about the Church of England. I wish you would put your suggestions forward.' What precisely were these?

The special session of the Ripon Diocesan Conference held in Harrogate on 10 December 1968 revealed all. It was devoted to the one issue of '*not* whether or not we want a union between the Church of England and the Methodist Church in this country, but whether we think that the plan now before us is the *right* way to achieve it'. Carefully taking members through the four questions on which their votes must be cast, John then expatiated on *The Bringing Together of the Ministries* section of the Service of Reconciliation. 'At this point the Commission was faced with a most difficult task – namely, to produce some rite, some form of word and action, which would be equally acceptable to those who think that the service *must* be treated as an ordination (or it is no use having it) and those who think it can't be so treated (or they would refuse to take part in it).' Various attempts to find the right formula had resulted only in a service which was 'deliberately vague and possibly ambiguous. Those taking part are invited to leave the question as to what is happening an open one, and to put everything in the hands of God.' Although this required an act of faith in God who would make up whatever was lacking in each, the real issue of differing concepts of the ordained ministry was being shirked. 'I believe that the whole doctrine of ministry and of priesthood in the Church of England is at stake at this point, and if we allow our doctrine of ministry to be diluted or impoverished we may be creating divisions rather than union and making the final unity of the whole Christian Church more difficult than it is now.' There was, then, a larger context in which all this must be seen, and he reiterated his oft-expressed belief that 'Unity is not like a jig-saw puzzle, where any joining-up of pieces is a step towards the whole. The problem is much greater than that, and the balance of one scheme over against other schemes has to be considered.'

Anxious, then, to avoid such 'papering over the cracks' as would in the end be 'a disservice to unity as a whole', he expressed his belief that 'union is not something that can be created, but something into which we must grow'. Consequently he urged a 'much more vigorous effort in the process of growing together'. Observing that little in this respect had been achieved during the 15 years that the Commission had been at work, he suggested the following programme:

I would like to see the two Churches to agree, as soon as possible, on the new Ordinal, and so start to build up a united ministry acceptable to all.

I would like them really seriously to work together during the next few years – e.g. in devising forms of government, in evangelism, in mission, in educational matters, in worship, and above all, in theological debate about such things as ministry and sacramental worship where I think we are deeply divided.

In an area where there is one Anglican church and one Methodist church, I would like it to become perfectly natural to have *one* joint evening service each Sunday, *one* Sunday School, *one* joint magazine, *one* Church Council, perhaps even *one* common fund.

So far as Intercommunion is concerned, I do not think that we could take away all barriers; but I would give a warm welcome to all baptized and practising Methodists to make their communion in our churches, if and when they wish to do so; and I would leave it to the conscience of each Anglican as to whether or not he made his communion in the Methodist Church.

Above all, he wanted to get rid of 'this highly emotional atmosphere in which we are now living', the regrettable language used by opponents in the debate, and the claim that the Holy Spirit belonged to one side only.

The Church press and the *Yorkshire Post* reported this faithfully, resulting in Archbishop Ramsey writing to ask for clarification on what he saw to be 'very near to indiscriminate intercommunion without any rectification or uniting of ministries', and also asking, 'Do you really think it is likely that the Methodist Church will accept episcopacy and a rule of episcopal ordination quite apart from any accompanying action to bring about full communion?' He added that of course he was 'giving much thought to what shall happen if the proposals break down... Inevitably we shall look to the people who while rejecting the present proposals keep telling us that there are better ways, and what would you say to a Commission of three persons, Lord Fisher of Lambeth (in the chair), the Bishop of Ripon and Mr Duffield [a leading Evangelical layman]. There is a prospect for you!' It would seem that the Archbishop was more than a little touchy on the subject, as John was only expressing his unhappiness with certain aspects of the proposals and not any opposition to the idea of reuniting with the Methodists. Undoubtedly Ramsey was staking a great deal on the success of the Scheme and was particularly offended by the discourteous opposition, publicly expressed, to it by his predecessor, Geoffrey Fisher. One bishop referred to this as 'Geoffrey-allergy'.

Ramsey's sensitivity in the matter did not diminish over the years. Nor, it must be admitted, did John's sense of grievance that he was not only being misunderstood but also that he was being stifled, as at Lambeth 1968. When the Scheme was voted upon in July 1969, only 69% of the Church Assembly voted in favour, thus falling short of the 75% required, while the Methodists more than achieved this with a 77.4% vote. Feelings ran high, and in particular many felt that the Methodists had been 'let down'. However, there was hope that with the replacing of the Church Assembly by the new General Synod in 1970 another attempt could be made to secure the necessary majority. The matter thus came to its final vote in May 1972. Ramsey spoke powerfully at the beginning of the debate for 25 minutes, followed by John who did not expect to be called so soon and as it were to lead the opposition. He was allocated only 10 minutes. Then at the end Ramsey emotionally exclaimed, 'Long live God. Long live God.' Even so, only 65.81% voted in favour, with six bishops now, instead of only two previously, voting against. 'The Scheme was dead', comments Professor Owen Chadwick,[48] boredom rather than bitterness having killed it. It was to be regarded as 'the one big failure' of Ramsey's life. John, however, agreed with Bishop Cyril Bulley of Carlisle that though the Scheme offered 'no through road to unification' this did not mean that there was no way of getting there at all. So he reiterated his conviction that the way to unity was not by paper schemes but by growing together. 'Unless we are prepared *now* to do *all* that is allowed, we are certainly not ready to go into organic unity.'

Unity was not to be achieved by partial unions, and growing together, not schemes, must be the basis of ecumenism. But more than that there must be a growing into Christ, as he was to say ten years later in Assisi. The occasion was the eight-hundredth anniversary of the death of St Francis, when he read a paper on 'S.Francesco e l'Ecumenismo'. 'The nearer we are to Christ the nearer we are to one another. Unity is not horizontal but vertical. Unity with Christ, in God, by the Holy Spirit, must come first. Our divisions are due to our failure to follow Christ literally. This is the great truth which Francis showed to us.' Then he quoted from Vatican II's *De Ecumenismo*: 'Let all Christ's faithful remember that the more purely they strive to live according to the Gospel, the more they are fostering and even practising Christian unity', adding that 'These words sum up what Francis did for ecumenism'. They could likewise sum up his own efforts for the cause which had dominated the last 25 years of his own ministry.

## Notes

1. *Ad Petri Cathedram*, 1959 (printed in *Acta Apostolicae Sedio* 51 1959, pp. 497-531).
2. *Vatican Observed, An Anglican Impression of Vatican II*, (Darton, Longman and Todd 1967). p. 27
3. The others were Professor F. C. Grant of New York and the Ven. Harold de Sousa, Archdeacon of Colombo. Canon Bernard Pawley also attended as the Archbishops' representative in Rome.
4. Later he contributed to *Vatican II by Those Who Were There* (ed. Alberic Stacpoole; Geoffrey Chapman 1986.)
5. *Vatican Observed*, p. 26.
6. Address to Ripon Diocesan Conference, October 1962.
7. *Vatican Observed*, p. 34.
8. Ripon Diocesan Conference, November 1964.
9. O. Cullmann, *Dialogue on the Way* (O. Cullmann, 'The Bible in the Council' in *Dialogue on the Way* ed. G. A. Lindbeck, Minneapolis, 1965), p. 136.
10. *English Bishops at the Council: Third Session*, p. 105.
11. Happily, 30 years later, the chalice is now generally offered to the laity.
12. *Vatican Observed*, p. 201.
13. 'One Fold or One Flock' in *Churchman* 91. 2 (April 1977), pp. 152–5.
14. R. H. Lightfoot, *St John's Gospel*, (Oxford University Press, 1956) p. 320.
15. *Vatican Observed*, p. 83.

16. B. C. Pawley (ed.), *The Second Vatican Council: Studies by Eight Anglican Observers*, p. 112. (Oxford University Press, 1967.)
17. *Vatican Observed*, p. 100.
18. See *Vatican II by Those Who Were There*, pp. 163, 167.
19. *Vatican Observed*, p. 111.
20. X. Rynne, *The Third Session: The Debates and Decrees of Vatican Council II*, (Faber and Faber, 1965) p. 2.
21. *Vatican Observed*, p. 145.
22. The encyclical *Humanae Vitae* of 25 July 1968 in the event condemned all forms of birth control except the 'rhythm method'.
23. *Vatican Observed*, p. 164.
24. *Vatican Observed*, p. 174.
25. *Vatican Observed*, p. 180.
26. B. Pawley and M. Pawley: *Rome and Canterbury through Four Centuries* (Mowbrays, 1974), p. 352.
27. Reprinted in Alan Clark and Colin Davis (eds.), *Anglican–Roman Catholic Dialogue* (Oxford University Press, 1974) pp. 1–2.
28. Hastings, *A History of English Christianity, 1920–85*, (Collins, 1987) p. 570.
29. Quoted in Clark and Davis, *Anglican–Roman Catholic Dialogue*, p. 14.
30. Purdy, *The Search for Unity*, p. 107.
31. Hastings, *History*, p. 569.
32. Malta Report III 20.
33. Purdy, *The Search for Unity*, p. 113.
34. October 1968.
35. Resolutions 52–4.
36. May 1968.
37. Hastings, *History*, p. 571.
38. Purdy, *The Search for Unity*, p. 126.
39. Purdy, *The Search for Unity*, pp. 128-29.
40. Preface to Authority in the Church I, in *Final Report*, p. 49.
41. *Final Report*, p. 50.
42. Authority in the Church II, in *Final Report*, p. 98.
43. Hastings, *History*, p. 645.
44. ARCIC I Final Report, p. 99.
45. Hastings, *History*, p. 565.
46. Hastings, *History*, p. 541.
47. Hastings, *History*, p. 568.
48. O. Chadwick, *Michael Ramsey: A Life* (Clarendon Press, Oxford, 1990), p. 341.

# 8

# Retirement in Durham

Although for so much of their lives John and Mary had regarded the Lake District as their natural home, it was not to be the place of their retirement. John felt that Mary should make the choice of where they should go, since for the 45 years of their married life so far they had always had to live where his work lay – in a tied house, moreover, not one of their own choosing.

Mary's choice of Durham was sensible: there was a fine cathedral with its round of well-sung services based on the Prayer Book; there was a university, so there would be access to libraries and contact with scholarly people; and, above all, it was in the north of England. It had a good rail service to London and easy access to the Lakes and the Trevelyan family homes in Northumberland. During the move they were able to have meals at Trevelyan College in Durham, of which Mary was already a Governor, and kindly neighbours called, including Alec Hamilton, then Bishop of Jarrow. John did not want to be involved in episcopal work in the diocese, and he felt that 'there are plenty of clergy here to preach at Harvest Festivals and the Mothers' Union'. Yet he needed to feel that he belonged somewhere without commitment – 'somewhere to hang up his cassock'. His neighbour in Springwell Road, Don Wilson, with whom he quickly struck up a friendship based on their common literary interests, took him to the 8 o'clock Communion service at St Oswald's, a church with a long Tractarian tradition. Its vicar, Gordon Roe (later Bishop of Huntingdon) was also rural dean. Having taken John on 'a quick verbal tour' of the city's churches, Gordon then invited

John to help him at St Oswald's. Here John regularly assisted as an 'episcopal curate' at the said BCP service on Sundays at 8 am, alternately celebrating and assisting with the chalice. On the latter occasions, however, he insisted on sitting in the choir to absolve and to bless. When Gordon argued gently with him about this, John insisted that it was a matter of order and not authority. However, when John wanted to wear his mitre, Gordon was equally insistent that he should not do so. Soon afterwards, however, he did invite John to preside in full episcopal robes at a Sung Eucharist. Even then John confessed to feeling lost without his pastoral staff.

It was not only the loss of episcopal dignity that John felt so keenly, but also the gossip about people and what was happening in the Church. He loved to be able to talk to Gordon Roe about bishops and Popes and the books that he was writing; he also enjoyed telling small groups of students about his time in Rome; and he corresponded regularly with old students from Chichester and former clergy, delighting in their visits and the chance of walking out in his corduroys with them from his 'sub-rural' home, or further afield. He would make enquiries about ageing clergy and old friends in Ripon, particularly Kenneth Lee and Lewis and Maysie Milnes whose declining faculties concerned him. But he never interfered in his old diocese, even when he was distressed to learn of the serious illness of his successor, Hetley Price, who tragically died of cancer in March 1977, less than a year after his enthronement. Thus only 15 months after John's retirement the diocese was again bereft.

John's own health, despite intermittent concern about his heart, had always been good, so that he was able to boast later that year that he had managed to live for 72 years 'without having ever had to go into hospital or be given a general anaesthetic'. But in June 1977 he had to have a prostate operation, followed by a further one a month later. Although the Dryburn hospital in Durham was not far from where he lived, he did not much enjoy the experience of being in what he called an 'old men's home' where the television was on all day. It was 'odd to be in a place with no clothes, no money, no keys – just in the hands of the medical staff', who impressed him with their cheerful and unstinting care. Here was an example of 'the world as it ought to be, not as it is... No-one was there to make money. No-one tried to get his own way regardless of the needs of others... Love in the biblical sense of the word was the overriding concern.' He was grateful for his few visitors, not least the Bishops of Jarrow and Knaresborough, the latter coming up from Harrogate to see him even though he had the full responsibility for the Diocese of Ripon at the time. The experience led him to write for the Ripon monthly newsletter, in which he urged clergy not to neglect their parishioners in hospital. 'Remember that what people suffer from most in hospital is not pain or discomfort but boredom,' he wrote. 'It is not necessary to talk about religion, but a man or a woman will be greatly comforted by a visit from someone representing the world outside the hospital.'

He was glad to get back to his home and his garden in Springwell Road, for he had been concerned about Mary being there on her own. As Alan Piper discerningly observed many years later – at Mary's funeral – a major part of John's ministry in Durham was as husband. Only he could drive the car, which he much enjoyed doing, not least for their regular shopping expedition to Framwellgate. He looked after their finances, but above all he engaged Mary's mind. Together they had literary interests in common, as well as ornithological, and their politics were similarly left of centre. In life John perhaps did more of the talking, but after he had died Mary found herself still talking a lot to him. Sad though their childlessness had been, not least in their declining years, there was no doubt that there had always been a 'marriage of true minds' and that it was deepest in the Durham years.

John, though, was the one who went out much more: in the diocese he served on the Advisory Committee and particularly enjoyed its outings to various churches; in the wider Church he continued for a further two years as Chairman of the

Advisory Committee for Religious Communities, as well as being Visitor of the community at All Hallows Ditchingham. He took on the presidency of the Henry Bradshaw Society from 1977, first assuring himself that it had a real continuing function in the editing of rare liturgical texts which would not otherwise have been published. So far from helping it to 'wind up' as he feared, he helped its officers to consider how they might celebrate the Society's centenary in 1990, although he himself did not live to see it. Above all, though, he remained a member of ARCIC I until the completion of its work in 1981 (see pp. 113–22). This was marked by his being presented with the Cross of the Order of St Augustine of Canterbury at Lambeth Palace on 1 September that year. Nearer home, he had set up an informal 'mini-ARC' group which met alternately at Yorkshire venues like Ampleforth and the Wood Hall Centre near Wetherby, while Durham and Ushaw College were the northern ones. Abbot Basil Hume was a member until moving to be Archbishop of Westminster in 1977, as was Canon John Fenton, Principal of St Chad's College, Durham until his move to Oxford in 1978. Bishop Gordon Wheeler of Leeds and Monsignor Buckley from Wood Hall were among the Roman Catholics who attended, while Professor James Atkinson of Sheffield, a noted authority on Luther, was one of the Anglicans. Fenton confesses that he felt somewhat of 'an outsider, a member of a different religion'[1] when the Roman Catholics were anxious 'to be absolutely clear what *authority* the meeting had', dismissing him perhaps as 'a liberal, and therefore of no standing'. But he greatly valued John's ability to convene such a diverse group, and the friendly atmosphere of their discussions.

John's main occupation in retirement, however, was in the study lined with some 5000 books, which also housed his grand piano and record-player, both of which he played most days, with Bach and Mozart predominant on the former and string quartets on the latter. Here, in what he called 'his part of the house', he continued the laborious work on *Medieval Franciscan Houses*, which was published by St Bonaventura's

University, New York, in 1983. 'It will not be a very popular book,' he wrote to a friend, 'but I hope it will be useful (see p. 57).' Concurrently he was able to relieve what was something of a tedious slog by writing the book which was very close to his heart, *The Anglican Spiritual Tradition*. It had been commissioned in 1978 by Darton, Longman & Todd, who then published it in 1983. By that time, however, the Alternative Service Book of 1980 was in general use up and down the country, and liturgical scholars, working in conjunction with those of the Roman Catholic and other Churches, were already looking ahead to new rites, calendar and lectionary for the twenty-first century. Some reviewers consequently felt that the book had a somewhat passé and nostalgic feel about it and did not give sufficient attention to twentieth century Anglican writers such as Ramsey, Ecclestone and Vanstone. Its main thesis, however, was that the Bible, particularly in the Authorized Version of 1611, and the Book of Common Prayer of 1662, together formed the 'twin foundation-stones of Anglican devotion.' Through four centuries these had enabled the continuity of a distinctive spirituality. Thus Owen Chadwick commended its readability, 'rare in histories of spirituality'; its clarity of expression (the hall-mark of all John's writing); and its 'proper historical understanding of Anglicanism'. Then in his review for the *Journal of Ecclesiastical History* he wrote, 'The book is mellow and full of faith; a wise and experienced Christian man coming after years of thought to a view of the tradition which is both grateful and optimistic; a devout and intelligent Anglican who wants to tell what he has found at the heart of Anglicanism.' Equally appreciative, but with a more consciously ecumenical perspective, was Gordon Dunstan's review in *The Month*. He saw the book as being in line with ARCIC's determination 'to discover each other's faith as it is today and to appeal to history only for our enlightenment, not as a way of perpetuating past controversy'. So here was a history, not of politics, organization or disputed dogma, but of 'the modes in which the faith of the Church of England has been expressed'. Both these scholars, then, regarded the book as a fitting epitaph for a man who was quintessentially Anglican.

These two were to be the last major books that John wrote, though he projected two others: neither attracted any of the publishers whom he approached about them. One was a collection of biographical sketches of six people who had influenced his life – Professor A. J. Grant of Leeds, Walter Greatorex at Gresham's, Dr G. G. Coulton in Cambridge, Kitty Burns in Holbeck, Brother Douglas the Anglican Franciscan, and Bishop George Bell of Chichester. The other was a collection of essays on ecumenical, Franciscan and medieval topics, which were considered too diverse for publication, especially as the market was too uncertain for writings of this kind. So John's final tally was 15 books, not the 16 or 17 which might have been, and eight of them were on St Francis or Franciscan subjects. His writings, however, continued with shorter pieces for journals, and two notable contributions to compendia. One of these was on Franciscan Spirituality in 1986 for *The Study of Spirituality*, of which his old friend Cheslyn Jones was one of the co-editors; the other, which also appeared in 1986, was to the collection edited by Dom Alberic Stacpoole, entitled *Vatican II by Those Who Were There*. No other pair of themes could have provided a more fitting swansong.

Towards the end of each of their lives, John's sister Theo wrote to him a revealing letter: 'I think about us quite a lot these days and feel sad to think that, though we have known each other fairly intimately for 80 years I seem to know so little, really nothing, about your thoughts and beliefs and faith. I am afraid that it is unlikely that we shall ever meet again and even if we did I expect we should just enjoy each other's company and leave these things undiscussed. Do you think you could write something *for me* that would help? You are, I know, a very *reserved* person and I, sometimes, a very *embarrassed* one...' She then spoke of their different paths and gifts, he as historian and churchman, she as craftsperson moved by beauty and simplicity; but both of them owing so much to their mother's strong belief and quiet personality, influencing others much more by what she was than by what she *did*. Sadly, as the letter came at Christmastime 1988 it is unlikely that John was able to reply.

Earlier that year John had suffered a stroke, which restricted his movements and for a while hampered his speech. He hobbled about the house with a stick, relying on George Rountree, his gardener, to look after the 'Aga' twice daily and to drive him and Mary to the bank and the shops once a week. He had always been concerned that he should not be 'the one to go first', as he knew how dependent Mary had always been on him. However, he ensured that there was sufficient domestic help with Mary Jobling coming in to clean twice a week, and he took the courageous step of selling his car and leaving his affairs in good order. Just after Christmas 1988 he had a further stroke, though he managed to get to St Oswald's for the Feast of the Epiphany a few days later. Then for the last week of his life he was back in hospital, where the Vicar of St Oswald's, Ben de la Mare, ministered to him daily. Just before he died on 13 January 1989, with Mary sitting by his bed, Ben read – in Italian – St Francis's *Canticle of the Sun* and Sister Death was welcomed.

Through Cardinal Willebrands the Pope's condolences were conveyed by telegram to Mary and she was thrilled that the Archbishop of Canterbury telephoned her from Lambeth. A simple funeral, attended by the Bishops of Durham and Ripon, was held in St Oswald's Church, at which Bishop Michael Manktelow, who had been one of John's students at Chichester, gave an address. At a later service of thanksgiving in Ripon Cathedral, Bishop Ralph Emmerson expressed the feeling of the diocese in losing a much-loved pastor and teacher. Eight years later the chapel of unity in the Cathedral was restored in John's memory and his pastoral staff which had travelled so often all over the diocese is now displayed there.

Mary, of course, missed John's companionship terribly. Well over a year after his death she wrote, 'I simply cannot get used to his not being there. Often I think he is just in the next room, and then the shock comes and I know he is not. I have tried writing letters to him, but it didn't really work, and I talk to him quite often, which is better. But it is best perhaps to remember happy days and grand days (e.g. at Rome) that we had together, with wonderful people like George and Hetty Bell and various diplomats who were kind to us in Italy!' But she also found comfort in taking memories of Italy even further back to her father's books on Garibaldi, 'which are thrilling, though a bit difficult geographically (tho' Daddy provided excellent maps). But Garibaldi is now having a great time in Palermo, with British naval officers hovering round.' Mercifully she was enabled to go on living at Springwell Road for another five years, with various 'home helps' and nurses to get her up each day and put her to bed. Gillian Boughton then moved in to be with her at night and to read to her. Among the books and the pictures which she and John loved so much, Mary felt him still near and wrote her own tribute, entitled 'Requiem':

> So sweet a life for sure must be
> Safe in a deep eternity:
> A Light that makes high Heaven aware
> Of a new glory shining there.

*

Towards the end of his life John wrote in a letter to a Roman Catholic laywoman,

I was brought up in a rather evangelical home, where religion was regarded as a very personal affair – a matter of believing certain things – the existence of God, the divinity of Christ, the power of prayer – and of being in close touch with the risen and ascended Christ whom we were taught to love and obey. I don't remember any talk about the Church, though we accepted the Church of England as a reformed part of the Catholic Church and never for one moment thought of deserting her for any other community. It was only later in my life that I became interested in the nature of the Church; and, of course, in recent years (especially since 1962 when I went to Rome as an observer at Vatican II) I have become intensely interested in what the Church *is*. In fact the *Constitution of the Church* (*Lumen Gentium*) comes very near to what I believe about the Church when it says: 'God has gathered together as one *all* those who in faith look upon Jesus as the author of salvation and the source of unity and peace, and has established *them as the Church*, that for each and all she may be the visible sacrament of this saving unity (his italics).'

Here is an eloquent statement not only of how one man's religion and thinking had developed, but also of how far the whole Church of God had moved in the twentieth century towards the recovery of its pristine unity in the One Lord. The accretions of centuries were being stripped away and divergences of history healed in the reassertion of simple yet essential truths. How Franciscan was this simplicity, how fulfilling of the saint's response to the Dominical command 'Rebuild my Church'. In a very real sense John Moorman's whole work as Franciscan scholar, teacher of the Faith, trainer of ordinands, shepherd of souls, bishop in the Church of God and ecumenist, had been to this single end – the building up of Christ's Church on secure foundations. It had required intelligence, independence and intrepidity; clarity of thought, conviction and courage. As with St Francis it had meant being a protester: so John protested against ecclesiastical introspection, the fudging of issues, and that faith in conferences, committees and schemes which characterized the Church of his day, hindering its effectiveness in that atmosphere of 'instability, permissiveness and affluence'² which pervaded modern society.

Anglican, Franciscan and Independent, John could at the end say with St Francis, 'I have done my duty: may Christ teach you yours.'

*Notes*

1. letter to author.
2. *A History of the Church in England* (3rd edn. 1973), p. 436.

# Bibliography of John Moorman's Writings

## A. Books

*Sources for the Life of St. Francis*, (Manchester University Press, 1940; reprinted by Gregg Press, Farnborough, Hants, 1966)

*Church Life in England in the Thirteenth Century*, (Cambridge University Press, 1945)

*A New Fioretti: A Collection of Early Stories about Saint Francis of Assisi*, hitherto untranslated, (SPCK, London, 1946)

*B. K. Cunningham: A Memoir*, (SCM Press, London, 1947)

*Saint Francis of Assisi*, (SCM Press, London, 1950; new editions, SPCK, London, 1963 and 1976)

*The Grey Friars in Cambridge, 1225–1538*, (Cambridge University Press, 1952)

*A History of the Church in England*, (A & C Black, London, 1953; Second Edition, 1967; Third Edition, 1973)

*The Curate of Souls: Being a Collection of Writings on the Nature and Work of a Priest from the first century after the Restoration, 1660–1760*, (SPCK, London, 1958)

*The Path to Glory: Studies in the Gospel According to Saint Luke*, (SPCK, London, 1960)

*Vatican Observed: An Anglican Impression of Vatican II*, (Darton, Longman & Todd, London, 1967)

*A History of the Franciscan Order, From its Origins to the year 1517*, (The Clarendon Press, Oxford, 1968; reprinted for Sandpiper Books, 1998)

*The Franciscans in England, 1224–1974*, (Mowbrays, London & Oxford, 1974, with preface by Cardinal Heenan; reprinted, 1982, preface by Cardinal Hume)

*Richest of Poor Men: The Spirituality of St. Francis of Assisi*, (Darton, Longman & Todd, London, 1977)

*The Anglican Spiritual Tradition*, (Darton, Longman & Todd, London, 1983)

*Medieval Franciscan Houses*, (St. Bonaventure University, New York, 1983)

## B. Articles

'The Permanent Element in the Life and Teaching of St. Francis' in *Theology*, 19.112 (October 1929), pp. 204–9

'Forerunners of the Oxford Movement' in *Theology*, 26.151 (January 1933), pp. 2–15

'A Note on Self-Examination' in *Theology*, 28.165 (March 1934), pp. 165–7

'Early Franciscan Art and Literature' in *Bulletin of the John Rylands Library*, 27.2 (June 1943), pp. 338–58

'The Medieval Parsonage and its Occupants' in *Bulletin of the John Rylands Library*, 28.1 (March 1944), pp. 137–53

'In Commemoration of Archbishop Laud, Executed on Tower Hill, London, January 10, 1645' in *Bulletin of the John Rylands Library*, 29.1 (July 1945) pp. 106–20

'A. G. Little: Franciscan Historian' in *Church Quarterly Review*, 144 (1947), pp. 17–27

'The Country Parochial System. Some Counter-Reflections' in *Church Quarterly Review*, 145 (1947–8), pp. 192–195

'Edward I at Lanercost Priory, 1306–7' in *English Historical Review* 67 (April 1952), pp. 161–74

'The Foreign Element among the English Franciscans' in *English Historical Review* (July 1947), pp. 289–303

'The Estates of the Lanercost Canons, with some notes on the history of the Priory' in *Cumberland & Westmorland Antiquarian & Archaeological Society's Transactions*, 49 NS, (1949), pp. 77–107

'Some Franciscans of Carlisle' in *C & W Antiquarian & Archaeological Society's Transactions*, 49 NS, (1950), pp. 74–86

'Saint Richard of Chichester' in *Theology*, 56.392 (February 1953), pp. 51–4

'Archbishop Davidson and the Church' in *Theology*, 59.433, (July 1956) pp. 269–75

'Charles Gore and the Doctrine of the Church' in *Church Quarterly Review*, 158 (1957), pp. 128–140

'Bishops' in *Prism*, no. 64 (August 1962), pp. 28–30

' "His Name was John": Some Reflections on *The Journey of a Soul*' in *The Heythrop Journal*, 6.4 (October 1965), pp. 399–411

'Assisi after Forty Years' in *The New Franciscan*, 1.9 (September 1968), pp. 197–201

'Franciscan Ideals' in *The Franciscan*, 13.4 (September 1971), pp. 171–7

'Bibliotheca Franciscana' in *The Book Collector*, (Spring 1974), pp. 19–26

'The Franciscans in England, 1224–1974' in *The Ampleforth Journal*, 79 part II (Summer 1974), pp. 47–55

'G. G. Coulton: Historian and Controversialist' in *Annual Report of Friends of Lambeth Palace Library*, (1975), pp. 9–19

'A Papal Letter to the Friars of La Scarzuola in 1373' in *Archivum Franciscanum Historicum*, 69 (1976), pp. 469–71 (includes text of letter)

'Saint Francis in his Era' in *The Franciscan*, 18.4 (September 1976), pp. 193–6

'One Fold or One Flock' in *Churchman*, 91.2 (April 1977), pp. 152–5

'The Agony of St. Francis' in *The Franciscan*, 24.3 (September 1982), pp. 119–23

'Father Cuthbert: A Great Franciscan Scholar' in *Collectanea Franciscana*, 52 (1982), fasc. 1–4, Rome (1982), pp. 299–315

'Arthur James Grant (Professor of History, University of Leeds, 1897–1927): A Biographical Essay' in *Northern History*, 24 (1988) pp. 172–91

(posthumously) 'Some Franciscans in England' in *Archivum Franciscanum Historicum*, vol. 83, (1990), pp. 405–20

## C. Contributions

'An Observer looks at the *Schema* on the Liturgy' in *Vatican II: The Theological Dimension*, *The Thomist*, 27, 1963

'The Ministry' in *The Second Vatican Council, Studies by Eight Anglican Observers*, ed. Bernard C. Pawley, Oxford University Press, 1967

'L'Espansione Francescana dal 1216 al 1226' in *Atti del IV Convegno Internazionale*, Assisi 1977

'The Anglican Bishop' in *Bishops, But What Kind?* ed. Peter Moore, SPCK, London, 1982

'Observers and Guests of the Council' in *Vatican II by Those Who Were There*, ed. Alberic Stacpoole, Geoffrey Chapman, London, 1986

'The Franciscans' in *The Study of Spirituality*, ed. Cheslyn Jones, Geoffrey Wainwright & Edward Yarnold, SJ., SPCK, London, 1986

Note: Moorman also wrote a Guide Book to Lanercost Priory, first printed in 1945; new edition 1976.

# Index